I dreamt I was a butterfly.

Now I am not sure
if I am a man dreaming
I was a butterfly
or a butterfly
dreaming I am a man.

— Chuang Tsu

Just get to the root, never mind the branches.

— Zen Master Ta Hui

The Butterfly's Dream

In Search of the Roots of Zen

by Albert Low

CHARLES E. TUTTLE COMPANY, INC.
Boston • Rutland, Vermont • Tokyo

Published in the United States in 1993 by
Charles E. Tuttle Company, Inc. of Rutland, Vermont &
Tokyo, Japan, with editorial offices at 77 Central Street,
Boston, Massachusetts 02109.

Library of Congress Cataloging-in-Publication Data

Low, Albert.
    [Rêve du papillon. English]
    The butterfly's dream : in search of the roots of Zen / Albert
Low.
        p. cm.
    ISBN 0-8048-1822-3 (pbk.)
    1. Zen Buddhism.   I. Title.
BQ9265.4.L6913 1993
294.3'42—dc20   93-16918
                                                 CIP

Credits and Acknowledgements:
p. 105: Excerpt from song ("Keep right on to the end of the road")
written and composed by William Dillon and Harry Lauder.
p. 114: Excerpt from song ("You are my heart's delight") from
"Yours is My Heart," music by Franz Leher, lyrics by Karl Farkas,
Ira Cobb, Harry Graham.
p. 127: Excerpt from song ("You stepped out of a dream") music by
Herb Brown, lyrics by Gus Kahn.

Cover design by Lisa Diercks

First printing 1993
Printed in the United States of America on acid-free paper.

Contents

Introduction

> Non-ambiguity and non-contradiction are one-sided and thus
> unsuited to express the incomprehensible.[1]

In his book *Meetings with Remarkable Men,*[2] Gurdjieff tells the following story. A man with a wolf, a sheep, and a cabbage had to cross a river. His boat could only carry himself and one other. How was he to get across without losing one or other of his charges? If he left the wolf with the sheep, he'd lose the sheep. If he left the sheep with the cabbage, he'd lose the cabbage.

It is not always the simplest and most direct solution that is the best, because to get out of his bind the man would have to make an extra crossing.

In the 1960s the acronym KISS was much beloved of managers, particularly those who were against too much thinking. KISS, in plain English, meant "Keep it simple, stupid." However, it so often happened that management seminars, in their endeavor

---

1   C. G. Jung, *Psychology and Alchemy,* trans. R. F. C. Hull (London: Routledge and Keegan Paul, 1953), p. 15.

2   G. I. Gurdjieff, *Meetings with Remarkable Men* (New York: Dutton, 1969).

to KISS, became so banal, trite, and tasteless that they were like salt that had lost its savor. Again, quoting Jung, "Scientific integrity forbids all simplifications of situations that are not simple."[3] This trying to make simple what is not inherently so is also a problem when trying to unravel the ambiguities and dilemmas of the subtle and mysterious realm of the human spirit.

Another story might help one see what I mean. A man lost his key and spent a long time looking around under a lighted lamppost for it. A neighbor who observed him for a while decided to help and joined the search. After five minutes or so the neighbor said, "Are you sure you lost it here?" "Oh no!" replied the man. "I lost it over there in the bushes." "Then what are we doing here; why don't we go and look there?" "Don't be a fool!" said the man, "There's no light there."

When we keep things brief and simple, there is clarity and we can work in the light. But sometimes it is not possible to work in the light, and then we have to go into the bushes.

The Question of Questions

The subtitle of this book is *In Search of the Roots of Zen*. To undertake such a quest it is not necessary to be a philosopher, nor what the world might want to call a "good person." What *is* necessary is to have a certain type of hunger, a hunger that must be satisfied in some ultimate way. This hunger is often accompanied by frustration and confusion that, if put into words, would sound something like, "What is life all about, what am I supposed to do, what is the good life?" And if one were to probe deeper still, "What am I, anyway!?"

----

3   C. G. Jung, *Psychology and Religion East and West*, trans. R. F. C. Hull (London: Routledge and Keegan Paul), p. 221.

"What am I, anyway?" sounds a bit strange because it gives expression to the deepest search that we have, and so we cannot ask it in words but only with the whole of our being. It is not simply a philosophical or psychological problem that we can hold at arms' length, but a concern underlying our whole life. A Chinese Zen master said that it calls for the concentration of "one's whole body, with its three hundred and sixty bones and joints and eighty-four thousand pores."[4] In the Bible the question came as a cry from the heart, "What is man that Thou art mindful of him?"[5]

I Think, Therefore I Am; or Am I?

Although it is not a philosophical problem, that does not mean that philosophers do not experience this hunger. For example, if you are familiar with Western philosophy, you know the saying of René Descartes, the seventeenth-century French philosopher: "I think, therefore I am." In his book *A Discourse on Method* he said that for some time he was filled with great doubt and constantly searched for some certainty by which he could escape from it. This great doubt is precisely the hunger that we are talking about. Descartes describes this state of hunger and confusion this way:

> [I am] filled . . . with so many doubts that it is no longer in my power to forget them. And yet I do not see in what manner I can resolve them; and, just as if I had all of a sudden fallen into very deep water, I am so disconcerted that I can neither make certain of setting my feet on the bottom, nor can I swim and so support myself on the surface.[6]

---

4   R. H. Blyth, trans., *Mumonkan* (Tokyo: Hokuseido Press, 1966), p. 32.

5   We use the word "man" as meaning "a human being" so we can stay within the context of the biblical saying. It is hoped that women reading the book will go along with this usage.

However, during his questioning, one thing he realized he *could* be certain of was that he was thinking, and so, in turn, he could have the further certainty "I am." His reasoning was something like this: "To doubt I must think; but to think I must be. I think, therefore I am." It has a certain guileless simplicity. But despite its simplicity, this phrase has created all kinds of problems, some of which we must talk about because they will help us bring out more clearly the real question at issue.

The Ghost in the Machine

Since Descartes' time, and to some extent because of his famous phrase, "I" came to be seen as a kind of ghost in a machine, the machine being the body and, by extension, the world. Furthermore, it has been believed by many of the best Western thinkers that the world is ruled by inexorable and eternal laws, laws, moreover, that human beings can know. At first these laws were seen as proof of divine intelligence, but gradually the divinity as well as the intelligence were ignored or rejected, and the metaphor of the machine took hold completely.

But even so there is this "I" that does not fit in the machine. It seems to have a life of its own, with free will, choice, values, and so on, and therefore, it seems to contradict the machine theory and all it stands for. The power of the machine metaphor was so great, however, that "I" was reduced to a disembodied ghost within. As one well knows, a machine has to be predetermined and predictable in its functioning, and all its parts interconnected. Therefore, free will, choice, decision, and judgment, because they are unpredictable, and because no connecting link can be found between them and the machine, have become more and more

---

6   René Descartes, *A Discourse on Method*, ed. Joseph Epstein (New York: Washington Square Press, 1965), p. 20.

suspect. So then people began to wonder what is the connection between the ghost and the machine.

Some thinkers denied the ghost any existence and said only the machine has reality. If the world can be understood as a machine, why bother with ghosts? "I," consciousness, memory, freedom, dignity, it was said, are all needless assumptions and can be discarded without doing any damage to the machine theory. This is a very simple, logical solution. If one accepts it, many unanswerable problems and unresolvable dilemmas go out the window. But, alas, so does all that makes our life worthwhile, such as meaning, freedom, creativity, love, and hope of a spiritual life.

Others went in the other direction and denied the reality of the machine. They said the whole thing is a dream, an illusion. This too has a beguiling simplicity, and, like the machine theory, cannot be argued away. It is, to use a formal expression, logically consistent. Perhaps you have played the game of asking someone, "Prove to me that you exist and are not simply the result of my imagination." No matter what the other says, the retort can always be, "But how do I know that too is not simply my imagination at work?"

The machine-only theory became known as *behaviorism* and is widely accepted as a theory, particularly in North America, although very rarely, if ever, is it accepted as a way of life. It is related to the view that conditioning forms the basis of human behavior and personality. In this view therefore, it is possible to control much of human development through the proper application of conditioning. The pain and pleasure of life, the way we relate to others, the way we love or hate, all this, it is said, is acquired through conditioning. The "I," if it exists at all, does so as the sum total of all the scribblings that life makes on the originally clean slate.

The second theory that the machine does not exist except as an illusion is, in its most extreme form, known as *solipsism*. Solipsism is very rarely held seriously even as a theory. A variation of it goes under the title of idealism, according to which the source of reality is an idea, and all that flows from the idea is but a construct of the mind. This would include the machine. Idealism has had much support from some of the finest minds, both Western and Eastern. However, it, too, is rarely accepted as a way of life.

Yet another alternative has it that both the ghost and the machine are equally real and continue along parallel tracks, so to speak. What is interesting about this is that, although it is very rarely accepted as an explicit theory, riddled as it is with problems, it is almost universally accepted as a way of life. Almost all live their lives as though they were a ghost in the machine, believing that they are personalities, persons, or souls, that they are individuals and real, but not material. In other words, they believe that they inhabit a physical body, ruled by physical and chemical laws, that behaves like a machine. Some go further to believe that this soul or personality might even reincarnate in a succession of bodies. Others, while denying previous existences, nevertheless feel that this ghost, or soul, goes somewhere, to heaven, they hope, after death. Yet others deny this and feel that the person, or personality, dies or is destroyed at death even though up to the point of death it has had a life distinct from the body. (At least they believe this until death whispers in their ear.)

Of course, few people, other than professional philosophers, worry their heads much about this problem in the way that I have described it, preferring to get on with the business of living and paying the bills. Until, that is, an itch begins to itch. They then try to scratch it.

"I" as a Magnetic Center

Suppose a man is making his way through a very dense forest. Suppose also he is a city dweller with no experience in the backwoods, and anyhow, because the forest is so dense, it is difficult, if not impossible, to find the sun or stars. He does, however, have a compass and knows he has to go due north to find his way out of the forest. Getting out of the forest is hard work. Often, it is necessary to back-track, make detours, and so on, to get around obstacles. It may be necessary to hack through the undergrowth, or to look out for snakes, bugs, and predators. Even so he is confident that it is only a question of keeping going, a question of time, and eventually he will get out.

But, now suppose he loses confidence in the compass. Maybe he begins to wonder, "How do I know it always points to the north? Perhaps it sometimes points to the south. Maybe after all I am simply going round and around in circles. It could well be I shall never find my way out!" Whereas, before the doubt set in, he only gave the compass a cursory glance to reassure himself of his direction, now he becomes obsessed by it. He studies it, examines it, thinks about it, shakes it, invents theories about it.

Quite likely nothing is wrong with the compass, at least not before he started shaking it and poking it around. But, now he can find no reassurance and so he becomes anxious, depressed, panicky. He wastes a lot of energy in tension, in running around getting lost, and trying to think his way out of the difficult situation he finds himself in. Even if he has all kinds of compasses, and books about forests and cosmology, he can find no peace. Even if someone were to write, "The compass points to the north and therefore, the north exists," it would make no difference, because the question would abide, "But does the compass point north?"

Our life with all its contradictions and confusions is, in a way, like a forest. But while we have a secure point of reference, which we call "I," we get down to the hard work of finding our way through the confusions. What happens if we lose this point of reference? It is then the itch begins, very often as a floating anxiety, an incipient panic, a terror or dread of something indefinable. We say we are afraid of this or that illness, or of madness, or of losing our job, or of losing a loved one. All these, however, are but symptoms of a more profound problem: the problem of no longer having an orientation point, or no longer having faith or confidence in what has so far served as an orientation point. The "I am" is in doubt. Identity crisis, some people call it; others call it empty nest syndrome, menopause, mid-life crisis. It can strike the young, the middle-aged, and the old. In the extreme, people break down, commit suicide, take drugs, become drunks, promiscuous, irresponsible.

"Who am I?" is now no longer a question to be asked in an ivory tower; one asks it, inexpressible and dreadful, at two o'clock in the morning, with a pounding heart and pouring sweat.

Once we have asked the question, life is never the same. It is like having crumbs in the bed; we can never sleep soundly. We start to feel that we must do *something*. But what?

The Right Answer to the Wrong Question

To get a right answer one must ask the right question. Before the 1939-1945 war the French came up with the perfect answer to the wrong question. The answer was the Maginot Line, which was a long and complex system of concrete fortifications. It was a perfect answer to the question, "How does one avoid the terrors and tragedies of trench warfare?" But, it was the wrong question. The right one was, "How does one fight a highly mobile and fluid war?" Many businesses go bankrupt not because of inefficiency, poor financing, or even poor management. They do so because, like the French, they ask the wrong question.

This is the real liability of simple answers to the spiritual problem. They may be good answers in themselves; but if the problems to which they are answers are not complete, if the problems do not reflect the full ambiguity and subtlety of the circumstances, the answers will be of little value. To find perfect answers to the wrong question is like building on sand. Let us therefore take another look at the question, "Who am I?" so that we can be sure that not only is it the right one but that it is also complete.

The Two Levels of "Who Am I?"

"Who am I?" or, put biblically, "What is man that Thou art mindful of him?" is a fundamental question. However, there is a catch to it, and that is where we start getting into the bushes. The question has *two levels*. The first is "Who am I?" The second is "How is it possible to ask this question?" In the biblical question the first level is "What is man?" and the second level is, "How is it that Thou art mindful of him?" If we do not recognize two levels, we go astray right at the beginning of our search and come up with the right answer but to the wrong, that is, incomplete, question. In Zen it is said that a tenth of an inch is all the difference between heaven and earth. That there are two levels seems a small point. Indeed, it is almost universally overlooked, but it makes all the difference between heaven and earth.

The first level of the question can be answered in a theoretical, philosophical way. But, the second level throws us into a vortex in which we begin to doubt the compass itself.

When I ask "Who am I?" I do so against the background of knowing "I am." "I am" is a given, and it is the "who" I am that is in question. To ask the question, of course, as Descartes so rightly says, I have to be. But what does this mean; *what is this "I" that has to be?* What we are saying is *that which asks the question is itself in question.*

We have not yet entered fully into the bushes, however. We must take yet another step. All the world's great religions have promised that if we seek earnestly enough we will find what we seek. In a famous story a Hindu guru took his disciple into the sea and held his head under the water for a few minutes. When the disciple came up gasping for air, the guru said, "When you want the truth as much as you now want air, it will be revealed to you." In the New Testament Christ says, somewhat mildly in the circumstances: "Seek and ye shall find." But a monk asked a Zen master, "Where should I seek?" The actual words he used were, "Where is my treasure?" The master replied, "Your question *is* your treasure." It is not only, therefore, that that which asks the question is in question, but that *this question itself is the answer*.

Will you venture then into the bushes, through the vortex of ambiguity to your own true nature? We will try to explore this question in depth, seeing more and more deeply into its nature; and we will find that, if we seek deeply enough, the search is truly the answer. I cannot promise the journey will be easy; it can be difficult and trying. But, it could be rewarding. Many of the examples and stories that we use come from Zen Buddhism. It is not necessary, however, that one take up Zen Buddhism to follow the book. We are talking about the human situation, yours and mine, whatever our beliefs. Whether or not you have read a lot makes no difference. We are not presenting a theory involving hypotheses, deduction, logic, and so on. What is being offered is a *description* based simply on observation and insight. Later in the book we will ask you to let go of your normal way of thinking to make an exploration using some simple exercises, so that you, too, can make your own observations. First we must prepare the ground.

The Parable of the Ten People

Before continuing, and to put our whole journey into perspective, let me tell you a story:

Ten people had to cross a river swollen by floods. The crossing was very precarious. When they got across they decided to count their number to confirm all had made it. One of them stepped forward and counted. 1-2-3-4-5-6-7-8-9. There were only nine! Another stepped forward and counted—again, there were only nine. They were all bewailing the loss of one of their group when a stranger came along and asked them what the problem was. They said, "There were ten of us on the other side of the river and now, after a difficult crossing, there are only nine. We have lost one of our friends." The stranger said, "Let me count." So he counted, "1-2-3-4-5-6-7-8-9-10." They were so relieved that they continued their way rejoicing.

However, the stranger too was wrong. Can you see why? If you think there were really eleven when he counted, you too will be mistaken.

The mistake is that we always overlook the one who counts. If you overlook this one when you read the book you will not be able to understand some parts. But, can you count the "tenth" person? If so how?

Chapter 1
I Don't Know

Let me start by telling a few more stories. As we go along I hope you will understand why I tell them. The first is about a monk who went to a Zen master, made his bows as required by custom, and went to speak, when the master struck him. "Hey!" cried the monk, "why are you hitting me? I haven't even opened my mouth yet!" "What's the good of waiting 'til you have opened your mouth?" growled the master.

The second story is about another monk's visit to a master. This monk asked, "What is the truth?" The master answered, "Ask the wall." "I don't understand," said the monk. "I don't understand either," said the master.

The Monk and the Emperor

The third is a koan, one of the enigmatic stories used by Zen practicers. It is the first of a very famous collection of koans, called the Blue Cliff Record, that are used to deepen the practice of Zen. It involves a monk called Bodhidharma who, tradition tells us, was responsible for introducing Zen to China. Bodhidharma went there from India about A.D. 500 and was over a hundred years old when he undertook the journey. In those days of small wooden boats and poor food storage, such a journey must have been a very arduous affair. When he arrived, Buddhism had been in China for about five hundred years. However, it was an arid religion, philosophical, mainly followed by monks and nuns, and lacking any real human content.

The first thing Bodhidharma did on his arrival was visit the Emperor. This Emperor, whose name was Wu, had done a great deal for Buddhism. He had monasteries built, had translations made into Chinese of the Buddhist scriptures, had supported monks and nuns, and generally done much good work. His first question to Bodhidharma was, "What is the merit for this?"

In the East, as in the West, most people believed they would go to heaven for doing good and to hell for doing bad. For example, in Buddhism there is a school called the Pure Land School, whose followers believe in a *pure land*, a heaven in Western terms, and that devout and good people go there when they die. The Emperor, when he asked his question was undoubtedly seeking confirmation that he too would be rewarded in some way for his good work. "What is the merit for this?" he asked. Bodhidharma replied, "None, Sire!"

Bodhidharma was very courageous to stand up to the Emperor like this. The Emperor was a most august figure, semidivine, and surrounded by people who were there simply to do his bidding. Most would have flattered him, either for fear of the consequences if they did not do so, or in the hope of gaining some type of recognition. But Bodhidharma did not do that.

Why Bodhidharma said there was no merit in doing good deeds calls for deep meditation. For example, did he want to deflate the Emperor? It is unlikely, because the Emperor was not his student and was not asking for spiritual guidance. Zen masters did not go around deliberately hurting people. Did he mean it literally, there was no value at all in what the Emperor had done? Again, it is unlikely. The Emperor's works obviously had some value, and, anyhow, a basic teaching of Buddhism is the teaching of Karma: that good results flow from good action. Why would Bodhidharma have replied "None, Sire!"

The Emperor was himself confused and asked, "What do you mean?" You must put yourself in the Emperor's shoes. Suppose you organized Oxfam, the Salvation Army, and the Sisters of Charity and then asked someone, "What is my reward for doing all this?" When the person says, "None!" would you not feel confused?

"What is your teaching?" the Emperor asked. "What is the highest principle you teach?" With this question he hoped to find some way he might understand Bodhidharma's words, some context that would give those words meaning so he could accept what the monk said.

The answer came: "Vast emptiness, and not a thing that can be called holy." This dumbfounded the Emperor even more. There, in front of him, was a monk, a holy man. Yet this monk was saying the highest teaching he had to offer was, not that there were no *holy* things, that would be bad enough, but that there was *no thing at all* to be called holy.

The Emperor too, as well as Bodhidharma, must have been a brave man, because he tried again. "But are you not a holy man?" He must really have stammered over this question. He was like a man who was being swept out to sea by an undertow. Not only was he not receiving the obeisance that, as an Emperor, was his due, not only was he not getting respect and the promise of reward for his good works, but, now Bodhidharma was telling him nothing was holy because there were no things. So he asked, "Are you not a holy man?"

"I don't know," said Bodhidharma, and was silent.

It was obvious to both they were not getting anywhere together, so Bodhidharma, probably with considerable sadness, turned and left.

Later, after the Emperor had recovered, a courtier came and asked him, "My Lord, do you know who that man was?" "I don't know," said the Emperor.

The key question in this koan, and really the reason I have told it, is what is the difference between the "I don't know" of Bodhidharma and the "I don't know" of the Emperor?

As we said earlier, you will understand these stories as we go along, but give them some thought now. What are they getting at? Please do not think that this type of question is only of value for someone who has a specific interest in Zen. As we will see, they have a universal appeal.

Who Am I?

I give workshops at the Montreal Zen Centre roughly each month, and often start with these three stories. Usually my listeners are as dumbfounded as the Emperor. All three stories, in their own way, are saying the same thing. But to know what this "same thing" is, one must get away from using thought in the usual, habitual way. The stories are not riddles, nor can they be understood by an examination of the words they use. They are not nonsense, nor are they meaningless. Bodhidharma is not giving a philosophy; philosophers and others addicted to words, concepts, and theories may be the least able to follow his meaning.

To know what he means one must know *oneself*, that which is beyond all form, all words. You, the reader, are not a woman or a man, you are not a Canadian, American, English, or French person. You are not a body or a mind, a soul or a spirit. You are not a self or a Self. You are not a ghost or a machine. You are not a human being and you are most surely not nothing. What then are you? What is the one who is never counted?

To penetrate Bodhidharma's "I don't know" is to penetrate the question "Who am I?" Normally, when people approach such a question as "Who am I?" they ask, "What kind of *thing* am I?" The idea I am a thing, a soul, a spirit, or a mind, or even just simply a body, comes naturally as a response to this type of question. Bodhidharma's "I don't know" cuts through all this. "I" am beyond all form, beyond all things. What does that mean?

4

Although I am beyond all form, simultaneously, I am also a collection of contradictory desires and wishes, hopes and expectations that clash and clang. This collection in Buddhism is called *karma*. I am my karma. On the face of it these two "I ams," "I am beyond all form" and "I am my karma," seem to be contradictory. On the one hand I am peace itself; to be beyond all form is surely to be beyond all conflict, all strife. On the other hand I am the essence of strife, indeed the essence of war itself; I am my karma means I am the swirl and grind of all that torments.

What Does It Mean, "I Don't Know"?

In *An Invitation to Practice Zen*, I invited readers to ask themselves why they were reading the book. I gave suggestions to help answer this question: one person might have been motivated by curiosity, another by the need to gain greater control over stress, another for reasons of physical or mental health. Others might have wanted to be more creative or have greater powers of concentration. All these can be gained to some degree or another by the practice of Zen, indeed, by the practice of many meditation practices.

However, I also suggested readers take another look and ask themselves whether this is really what life is about. Is life simply a series of having, and then satisfying, wants? If so, it is just an endless, restless treadmill on which we are condemned to labor.

One day a woman came to see me. She had made a long, tiring, and somewhat costly journey. I asked her, "Why have you come here?" Instead of answering she gazed out of the window; then, after several moments, she turned and gazed at me and, suddenly, burst into tears. While the tears flowed she looked through them at me and said, "I don't know what is happening to me. Why am I crying?" I asked her again gently, "Why did you come here today?" She broke down completely and sobbed, saying, "I don't know. I don't know. That is the trouble, I really don't know what I want!"

That was right. She did not know what she wanted.

But if so, why had she come so far? Why had she made all that effort and gone to all that expense if she did not know why? It is obvious she *did* know why. She must have done. Then why did she say she did not?

To help people attending a workshop understand this crucial point, which obviously has a bearing on the story about Bodhidharma and the other two stories, I ask them to raise their hand. When they have done so I ask, "Who raised the hand?" Generally, the reply is, "I did." Then I ask, "How? How did you raise your hand?" Dozens of muscles are used, all kinds of nerve pathways traversed. If "I" raise the hand, how is it I do not know which of these I use and when; how is it I do not know how I put them into action and how I stop them?

Other people say it is the body that raised the hand. I then ask, "Why? Why did the body raise the hand?" "Because you told it to," is often the answer. "But, if I tell it to jump off a cliff will it do so?"

There is some controlling factor, something that puts it all into action, something that chooses and decides. To call it mind or soul does not help. All that would be accomplished by doing so would be to substitute one unknown—mind or soul—for another. Even to say "something" controls is already too much. Is there "something"?

What is it that understands these words, what is it that sees the book, that hears noises when they occur, that tastes food, that thinks, loves, hates? Please ask yourself this question in all seriousness, if not now, then later, when the mood strikes you.

The only true response is, "I don't know." But what kind of "I don't know" is it?

The Many Faces of "I Don't Know"

Some people might feel, "Well, does all this really matter, is it not all philosophical and theoretical?" Yet our whole life and death are involved with this problem. That which moves, sees, and thinks, was it born, will it die? Is it in space and time? If not, then where and when is it? Do you not ask sometimes, "Why was I born? What is the meaning of my life? Where do I go to after death? Why must I suffer?" But who is it who was born? Who dies? Who suffers? Whose life does or does not have meaning? To say "I do," or "It is 'me' or 'mine'" is all right grammatically, but, again, what is this "I," this "me," this "mine"; *what, if anything, lies behind these words?*

There are several different ways of using the expression "I don't know." That is one of the things the story, the koan, is bringing to our attention. There is the "I don't know" of Bodhidharma, and the "I don't know" of the Emperor. For example, if I asked you, "What did I have for breakfast this morning?" you would answer, "I don't know." However, implied in this "I don't know" is the realization, "If I wanted to, I could find out." There is an ocean of things, of facts, like this that one does not know, but that nevertheless, if one wanted to, one could find out. For example, if I died suddenly, the police might become very interested in finding out what I had for breakfast.

You might ask a friend, "Who was the woman who just walked by?" Your friend might say, "I don't know." Then later the friend might come back and say, "That woman who passed us yesterday is a schoolteacher who just moved into the neighborhood." You would then feel you know who she is. That is how most of us use "I know—I don't know."

When the Emperor replied, "I do not know" in answer to the courtier's question, "Do you know who that man was?" he used the phrase in that way. "If I wanted to," the Emperor implied, "I could find out his name, where he came from, who sent him and so on. In other words, I could know who he is." Probably that kind of answer would have satisfied the courtier.

"I do not know a fact" is another use of "I don't know." This is apart from the use made of it by the agnostic. *Gnosis* means "knowing," agnostic means "not knowing." An agnostic is one who says he or she does not know the nature of ultimate things. For example, we have the theist who says God exists, the atheist who says God does not exist, and the agnostic who says human beings cannot know the answer to these things.

Do you think Bodhidharma was answering as an agnostic the question, "Are you a holy man?" Did he mean "I don't know. Human beings are unable to know"? If you asked someone, "Who raised the arm?" and he replied, "I do not know. Human beings are not able to know," would you not think such an answer strange? Would you not want to ask, "Who then are you who doesn't know?"

There is obviously another meaning yet to this "I don't know," and it is precisely that meaning we are talking about.

"I Don't Know" as Knowing

The word *Buddha* means awakened to not knowing.

To most people this will seem strange. It is well known that many men and women practice Zen for a number of years before coming to awakening. Why should they bother, if it is simply awakening to "I don't know"?

Buddha said:

> My Doctrine implies thinking of that which is beyond thought, performing that which is beyond performance, speaking of that which is beyond words and practicing that which is beyond practice.[1]

To think means to arouse the mind. To "think beyond thought" is to *arouse the mind without any limitation or obstruction. To arouse it without allowing it to rest on anything.* To "speak of that which is beyond words" is to speak of that which is beyond all formal knowledge, all theories and ideas. To do that which is beyond

---

1   F.L. Woodward, ed., *Some Sayings of the Buddha* (London: Oxford University Press), p. 17.

8

doing is to be totally free and spontaneous, to arouse the mind without resting it on anything.

Bodhidharma's not knowing opens the mind in this way, beyond the limits of any formal knowledge. It is also in this way one must understand why the master in the first story would say it is pointless to wait until the monk has opened his mouth to hit him. To speak, to ask a question, is already to have closed the mind. Even going to ask the question is to have closed the mind. But this does not mean that one has to take a vow of silence to know the truth.

Buddha also said:

> There is an unborn, unbecome, unmade, unconditioned. If there were not an unborn, unbecome, unmade, unconditioned, then we could not here know any escape from the born, become, made, conditioned.

> But, since there is an unborn, unbecome, unmade, unconditioned, then we know there is an escape from the born, become, made, conditioned.[2]

Japanese poet Basho wrote a haiku in which he sums up precisely these remarks of Buddha:

> No one
> walks along this path
> this autumn evening.

According to Zen, each of us is this unborn, each is this "no one." Whole and complete, lacking nothing in wisdom, compassion, and peace. To know this it is simply necessary to arouse the mind without resting it on anything. To arouse the mind without resting it on anything is to know, but not to know anything specifically.

---

2   *Ibid.*

This wholeness and completeness is our true nature, our true home. But if such is the case, why are we so far from peace? Why is there so much suffering and conflict, so many wars and revolutions, so much sadness?

In spiritual practice the truth of wholeness is the magnet that draws us on, while pain of separation is the goad that drives us. Let us continue and see if we can deepen our questioning.

Chapter 2
The Origin of Human Suffering

Ignorance

In the last chapter we said that Buddhism means awakening to "I don't know," to knowing without limit or definition. This knowing (which in Buddhism is called bodhi), along with compassion and peace, is our true nature. To say "I know who I am" would be to know something, someone; it would be to know a body or a personality made up of memories and expectations, ideas and preferences. But this is not who I am. I am not an idea or personality, I am that which knows I am. How can I know who I am? How can we know knowing? With what light would one look for the sun.

But as we have already asked, if our true nature is knowing, why are we so confused? If our true nature is love and compassion, why do we hate and fear one another, why do human beings do such terrible things to one another? If our true nature is peace, why do so many people spend endless nights in torment and endless days fearing tomorrow.

In the last chapter we quoted Buddha. On another occasion he said:

> There is that sphere wherein is neither earth nor water, fire nor air: it is not the infinity of space, nor the infinity of

perception; it is not nothingness, nor is it neither idea nor non idea; it is neither this world nor the next, nor is it both; it is neither the sun nor the moon.[1]

It neither comes nor goes, it neither abides nor passes away; it is not caused, established, begun, supported; it is the end of suffering.

In Buddhism the basic *defilement* is ignorance. Most of us associate ignorance with not knowing. One might wonder, if one did not understand the meaning of Bodhidharma's "I don't know," how it can be that one would practice for many years to awaken to "I don't know" if I don't know is a defilement! Perhaps we can spend some time considering this ignorance to see what it really means, as it will lead us into the heart of the human situation. But before we do so, let us talk about the word "defilement" and why it is used here in this expression of *defilement of ignorance*, as it will help us get our bearings.

Defilement and Sin

For many Christians the belief in sin, that human beings are sinful, is basic. This belief can create several problems for the Westerner who comes to practice Zen because in Buddhism it does not exist. As we just said, in Buddhism, ignorance is the basic *defilement*, not the basic *sin*. The word used in the original Sanskrit texts was *kleśa,* and some Western translators, because of their upbringing, automatically translate it as "sin" instead of "defilement." However, kleśa really means a situation that gives pain to others and to ourselves. As we will see below, there are three primary kleśa: ignorance, greed, and anger, and it is out of these three that what we know as *ego* arises.

---

1   Bikku Nananda, *Concept and Reality in Early Buddhist Thought* (Kandy: Buddhist Publication Society, 1971), p. 62.

Someone unsympathetic to the Christian religion might say that because of their belief in sin, Christians are at best mistaken, at worst deluded. Many people who have been brought up as Christians later in life reject the whole of Christian teaching, saying that it is obsessed by sin. Others may well wonder, thinking that if sin is a fact basic to the human condition, why is it that everyone does not share the belief of its existence?

Christians, on the other hand, might well say, and often do, that it is because Christianity is nearer to the truth than other religions, that the truth of original sin has been revealed to it. Therefore believing Christians have access to truth that is denied to nonbelievers, and are therefore aware of sin in a way that others cannot be. This is the position taken by the Roman Catholic Church. The coming of Christ, it says, was to proclaim the message of sin and the promise of redemption. Not to have received this message is a misfortune so great that it was formerly believed it would condemn one to everlasting damnation. This belief has been somewhat softened in more recent times.

However, a third alternative exists that we will adopt. According to this alternative, that which is basic to human nature is inexpressible, but so important to our well-being that human beings just *have* to find some way to give it expression and make it available to consciousness. The way it is expressed and incorporated into our consciousness will determine largely what sort of people we are, our morality, our way of dealing with others and with the world. One culture will find expression one way, another a different way.

Sin and Kleśa

In the West, particularly among those brought up in the Roman Catholic and Calvinist traditions, the belief in sin is deeply ingrained. For them, atonement for our sins is the raison d'être for the religious life, and the birth and death of Christ were the means by which humankind could be redeemed from original sin.

But, let us repeat, there is no notion of original sin as such in Zen Buddhism; however, there is something similar. There is kleśa.

What are the similarities and differences between Christian sin and Buddhist kleśa? Is it possible to find ways of talking about what underlies them both so it can become more understandable to us in present-day culture? Let us not fall into error and say that Buddhists and Christians are simply using different words for exactly the same idea, because if we do we might miss important differences between them. But also do not let us fall into the error of saying one is right and the other wrong. To do this would be to reject the beliefs and understanding of generations of devout and often deeply committed, intelligent people.

The Ignorance of Adam and Eve

The primary sin in the West is disobedience. Original sin comes from the disobedience of Adam and Eve. God told Adam and Eve they could eat of any fruit in the Garden of Eden but not the fruit of the tree of knowledge of good and evil. However, they ate this fruit and so were evicted from the Garden. This act of original disobedience was, the Christian religion tells us, the original fall from grace of human beings, and all of us share in the guilt and suffering that ensue. For the Church, it is essential that the idea of original sin be maintained, because redemption and salvation are possible only through the mediation of Christ, whose surrogate here on earth is the Pope and whose instrument is the Church of which he is the head.

All Beings Are Buddha

On the other hand a Zen Buddhist master said, "From the beginning, all beings are Buddha." This means that from the very beginning we are whole and complete. We have no need to be

14

saved. We already have all that is necessary for a life of peace, compassion, and wisdom. The Christian also believes something like this: Since Christ died for our sins, and provided this death were not simply a futile gesture, then all persons must be saved. That is similar to saying that all are whole and complete. Even some Catholics, for example, contemporary writer Matthew Fox, want to promote the teaching of wholeness and completeness, with its implication of joy and creativity. Fox says that this teaching is of more importance than the teaching of original sin, which implies suffering and sadness. However, the fact that the Church imposed a year of silence on him shows that original sin (in the eyes of the Church) is still a basis of Christian teaching.

Why Do We Suffer?

If for the moment we accept the Zen Buddhist teaching that we are whole and complete, the question then naturally arises, why is it that we suffer? Why are we anxious, depressed? Where does stress, the feeling of being overtaxed, burdened by life, come from? Why do we feel so guilty, so often ashamed of ourselves? Let us follow through the explanation that the Church gives, as this is familiar to most readers. Then we will be able to see how this relates to what we can learn from Zen.

According to the Church

Let us repeat, the Church says we suffer because of an original act of disobedience. Another way of putting this is to say we suffer because, by this disobedience, *we separate ourselves from God.*

There are two ways we can understand the word "God": as the Creator of the universe, in which case He stands outside creation; or as the ground of our being, and therefore instead of being remote, He is intimately and directly involved in this creation. This second way is the way, for example, St. John of the Cross understood the word God. He says:

15

> God dwells, or is present, substantially in every soul, even
> in the soul of the greatest sinner. This kind of union is never
> lacking since it is in and by this that He sustains their being.[2]

As we know, particularly if we are parents, disobedience is when someone says "No! I won't." If one accepts the second meaning of God as the ground of our being, then disobedience is saying No! to the most basic part of ourselves; we separate ourselves from that which is most essentially ourselves. Furthermore, with this No! as a foundation, we live and experience, form habits, and acquire beliefs. Our whole life then becomes estranged from its roots and from the ground of being. This estrangement moreover will have a characteristic feeling that we associate with guilt, angst, and suffering, feelings we so desperately want to appease.

According to Zen

Buddha, even while proclaiming that we are whole and complete, taught the "noble truth" of suffering. Indeed, he said that life is founded on suffering. This does not mean simply that suffering is the first experience we have in life. It means suffering is the very mortar that holds the edifice of life together. As we said, many people will object to this and say that it is not so, that happiness, even joy, is the basis of life. As we have agreed, they too are right, for "From the beginning all beings are Buddha." From the beginning all beings are happiness and contentment itself. Furthermore, as we also said earlier, we all know this. All of us, all the time, know this truth, and yet all of us, all the time, also know the truth that life is suffering.

How are we to understand this apparent contradiction?

---

2   St. John of the Cross, *The Dark Night of the Soul*, trans., abridged, and ed. Kurt F. Reinhardt (Frederick Ungar), p. 34.

Suffering arises, the Buddhist would agree, because of a fall from grace. It arises because of an original kleśa that is ignorance. Now ignorance does not mean illiteracy and cannot be remedied by studying and learning. On the contrary, although people so often resort to studying and learning because of ignorance, this simply compounds the problem.

It may be a happy coincidence, but in the very word "ignorance" lies its Buddhist meaning. To ignore is to reject part of a situation. For example, if I ignore you, I pretend you are not there. If I ignore a pain in the leg, I act as though the pain were not present. I know of course you *are* there, or the pain *is* there, all the time, even while I am ignoring one or the other. Your presence will affect what I do, think, and feel, but because I am ignoring you, *I will not necessarily be conscious of being so affected.*

A monk once said to a Zen master, "If it is true we are all whole and complete, why is it people do not know this?" The master replied, "They know it." *We all know it but we ignore it,* we pretend it is not so. But this does not mean that this knowing does not affect our lives. Christianity has a wonderful expression that says, "If you had not already found me, you would not be seeking me." How could we ever seek God if we had not already found God, or wholeness if we were not already whole? How could we seek peace if we did not already know peace, if peace were not already part of our being? But nevertheless we ignore our wholeness.

It is now obvious that the kleśa of ignorance, just as Christian disobedience, means a turning away from the ground of our being.

But why would we want to do such a thing?

The Buddhist reply is given in the second noble truth of Buddhism: "The cause of our suffering is desire." That is, because of desire we turn away from the ground of our being, and we do it through ignorance. The word used for desire is *trsna,* which can be translated also as thirst. Desire, greed, thirst, whatever word we use, is intimately bound up with ignorance. What is interesting is that in Genesis the cause of disobedience is *hunger* and, in this context, hunger and thirst mean more or less the same thing. Indeed, in the beatitudes Christ says, "Blessed are they who hunger and thirst after righteousness." To hunger and thirst after something is to desire it. Adam and Eve ate of the tree of knowledge of good and evil because they hungered after the fruit.

Understanding Adam and Eve

How then are we to understand this eating the fruit of the tree of knowledge of good and evil?

According to the Bible, God said:

> Of every tree of the garden you may freely eat but of the tree of the knowledge of good and evil you must not eat for the day that you do eat it is the day you shall surely die.[3]

What is the tree of knowledge of good and evil? Obviously there is no such tree, and so this must be an allegory. This allegory could be interpreted as God saying that you may satisfy all hunger ("Of every tree of the garden you may freely eat"), *except* if you have hunger for knowledge ("for the day that you do eat it is the day you shall surely die"). By knowledge is meant (because Genesis talks of the tree of good and evil) knowledge of opposites, good and evil, right and wrong, and so on.

It should be emphasized that God said knowledge will cause us to die. This can be understood to mean we die from the life of wholeness and are reborn into the life of separation and conflict. This death from the life of wholeness is but a more concrete expression for saying "we turn our back on it."

---

3   Gen. 2:16-17.

18

The Ignorance of Good and Evil

Zen masters say the same thing over and over: Judging good and evil is an obstacle to awakening. For example, a famous verse by the third Zen patriarch in China begins:

> The Great Way is not difficult
> For those who do not judge good and bad.
> When preferences are cast aside
> The way stands clear and undisguised.[4]

The Great Way is awakening: when we do not judge good and bad we are already awakened. As we have said, to judge good and evil, to eat the forbidden fruit, is to separate ourselves from the ground of our own being.

We judge good and bad because we hunger for the good. We hunger to *be* good, to *know* good, and to *own* what is good. Instead of "good" we can also say "right," "to be perfect," "to be excellent," and so on. We want to be right, or perfect, or excellent. Among the most painful things one can say to another is, "No! You are wrong!" or, "You are bad," which often comes across as, "You know, people don't like you very much." Or to tell them what they own is bad. We do not say to a neighbor, "You know your house is really quite ugly." We may think this, but we are far more likely to try to find something good to say about it and so improve our relations with the person.

Darwin and Genesis

A discussion flares up now and then as to whether Genesis or Darwin is correct. However, Darwin and the evolutionists are concerned with the origin of the human being; that is, with the

---

4   Hsin Hsin Ming, *Affirming Faith in Mind: Daily Chants and Ceremonies* (Rochester: The Zen Center, 1985), p. 16.

human *form*, which is but one form amid myriad forms. On the other hand, Genesis, with the story of Adam and Eve, is not so much concerned with the origin of the human *being* and its form as with the origin of the human *situation*. That is true of many myths. They are concerned with coming to terms with the human situation, its suffering, destiny, and meaning; few myths are simply forerunners of more sophisticated scientific understanding. If one reads Genesis carefully one sees it says very little about the origin of the human being; it gives but one sentence to the creation of man: "The Lord God formed man of the dust of the ground and breathed into his nostrils the breath of life." For the creation of woman it just says, ". . . and the rib, which the Lord God had taken from the man, made he a woman, and brought her unto him." But on the other hand it says a lot about the origin of the human situation and human suffering.

Plato's Myth

For those who like mythology, another myth that has a bearing on what we are saying was retold by Plato, the Greek philosopher. He spoke of a race of beings who had two heads, four arms, and four legs, and were so strong they were threatening to the gods. In their anxiety about this, the gods decided to cut these beings in half such that each had one head, two arms, and two legs. That was the birth of the human being. Ever since, we have wandered in search of our other half. Plato's wording is quaint and is worth repeating:

> Let us slice them through the middle. In this way they will be weaker and there will be more of them to do the work of the gods.

> Each of us is like half a person sliced through like a flatfish and two made of one. So each seeks the other half.[5]

It may be of interest to the reader to know a Jewish myth says something similar. Mircea Eliade, a Romanian mythologist, said:

> According to the Bereshit Rabba, "Adam and Eve were made back to back, joined at the shoulders; then God divided them with an axe stroke, cutting them in two."[6]

What these stories have in common is in their telling us we have turned our back or fallen from an original unity. Furthermore, the Zen Buddhist and the Bible both agree this happened through the hunger for, and acquisition of, knowledge. Another word that we could use instead of knowledge in this instance is *consciousness*.[7] It is because of the opposites, that is, good and bad, yes and no, that it is possible for us to be conscious, and it would be nearer the mark to say it was the desire for consciousness that made us to turn our back upon our original happiness and peace, our original wholeness. However the myth of Plato goes further and says that love

> seeks to renew our ancient nature in an endeavor to unite in one single being two distinct beings and therefore to restore human nature to good health.[8]

It says also that the soul of each lover "tends toward something *which it cannot express but which it feels and reveals mysteriously.*"

5   Plato *Symposium*, xiv-xv.

6   Mircea Eliade, *The Two and the One* (New York: Harper Torchbooks, 1965), p. 104.

7   The word conscious comes from two roots: *con*, which means "together" and *scio*, which means "I know."

8   Plato *Symposium*, xiv-xv.

The Common Origin
of Suffering and Consciousness

This turning our back, aside from being the origin of consciousness, is also the origin of our suffering. This is an important point and should be stressed in our psychoanalytically drenched society. If we accept the Buddhist teaching on suffering, it becomes apparent that suffering does not come from the kind of traumatic experiences that the Freudians speak of. It would therefore be a bit futile to try to find the origin of suffering in the past, be it a primal scene, castration fears, or the ineptitude of our mother while nursing us or while toilet training us. *We suffer because we are human.*

But we do not suffer in the abstract; our suffering is *experienced*, which is to say we grieve the loss of a friend, we are anxious about our health, we are depressed about lack of gratitude, and so on. Because we can only know our suffering *through* experience we believe it comes *from* experience. However, traumatic incidents merely provide the trigger and not the cause of the suffering, the cause being the initial separation from ourselves and the longing to return to wholeness.

From this point of view we can see the past as a reservoir of unsuccessful attempts to come to terms with suffering. This reservoir is important as it gives form to what otherwise would be an intolerable burden of inexpressible suffering. Indeed, it is possible some psychotherapy is successful precisely because it gathers together and gives sanction to these ways of giving expression to suffering. These psychotherapies, of which Freudian psychoanalysis is a good example, gather particular traumatic events and by interpretation and interpolation of theory, create with these events plausible vehicles by which suffering can be made conscious and thus controllable. Thus psychotherapy is really a way of creating custom-made myths by which one can replace the myths, rituals, and rites of passage of earlier cultures.

Let us pause for a moment and stress the importance of what we are saying about suffering. Both Christianity and Buddhism teach that it is not traumatic experiences that are the cause, but ignorance. For the Buddhist, ignorance is the origin of suffering: we ignore our true nature. For the Christian this ignorance is the original sin. But let us remember that by ignoring our true nature we do not dispose of it. Therefore, although ignorance is the origin, nevertheless the source of all, including ignorance, is this true nature. This is constant, immutable, never absent, unborn, and without death.

The Differences between Zen and Christianity

So far we have been at pains to show how alike Buddhism and Christianity are in the understanding they have of the origin of human suffering. But we must also stress the differences, because in them are found some of the obstacles many Westerners meet when trying to come to terms with the Buddhist way.

No Savior

The essential difference is that Buddhism has no concept of God as creator. Because there is no creator we cannot rely on God or on a messenger from God to save us. Each of us from the beginning is Buddha, and each of us in our turn is guilty of turning our back on this truth. Each one of us suffers the consequences. Each can have a change of heart, or, using a Christian word that is similar, *repent*. But no one can "purify," that is, save, another.

This is expressed very beautifully in a Buddhist text that says:

> By oneself evil is done
> By oneself one suffers
> By oneself evil is undone
> No one can purify another.

What this means in practical terms is each of us must take up our own Cross and do the work necessary for salvation. In the West, until fairly recently, this has been an unusual idea.

The Church formerly frowned on people finding their own way, and sometimes (for example, during the time of the Inquisition) went much farther than merely frowning. So there has been no systematic development of spiritual methods. This is not to say spiritual methods have not existed in the West, but they existed more as the exception and were practiced primarily in monasteries and convents.

No Miracles

Because we do not have a tradition of working on ourselves in a spiritual context, when we do hear about such work as meditation we tend to think that one must gain something from the practice. Coupled with romantic stories about the East, this has given rise in some people to all kinds of strange expectations and hopes. One well-known meditation system promised its followers courses on levitation, walking through walls, and omniscience. Recalling past lives, discovering hidden powers, mind reading, and channeling are offered by people drawing on the so-called secrets of the Shamans, the Native Americans, the Tibetans, and the Druids.

Humankind has always hungered after miracles. But our culture has nurtured this hunger. First through the Church, for whom the exemplar of the human race was a saint whose chief attribute was the ability to work miracles; and more recently through television commercials, whence come the gospels according to St. Big Mac or St. Coke, which say that with one bun, or bottle of fizzy liquid, one goes straight to heaven, boots and all. Buried deep in us is the belief we can change in miraculous ways anything we do not like both in the world and in ourselves. This has been aided and abetted by technology, as well as by some of the more modern psychotherapies where all that is necessary, according to one, is a good scream, or according to others, the patient putting into words what ails him or her.

True spiritual practice, however, West and East, is not founded on attainment or on the miraculous, but on seeing life itself as a true miracle. In the words of a Zen master.

> My magical power and miraculous gift:
> Drawing water and chopping wood.[9]

A Westerner might say: "My magical power and miraculous gift: putting out the garbage and washing the dishes..

The miracle is not that one can walk on water or through walls, but that "one" can walk, talk, hear, and see. To know this "one" is the greatest miracle of all. But to know it is not an attainment. Someone asked Dogen, a famous Japanese Zen master of the twelfth century, what he had gained from his long and arduous practice of Zen in China. He said, "I know my nose is vertical and my eyes are horizontal." Another master said that "everyday life is the way."

As T. S. Eliot said:

> We shall not cease from exploration
> and the end of all our exploring
> Will be to arrive where we started
> and know the place for the first time.[10]

---

9   Ruth Fuller Sesaki, Yoshitaka Iriya, and Dana R. Fraser, trans., *The Recorded Sayings of Layman Pang* (Weatherhill, 1971), p. 46.

10   T. S. Eliot, "Little Gidding," *Four Quartets* (London: Faber and Faber, 1954), p. 43.

Chapter 3
The Inner Contradiction

In the second noble truth Buddha said the cause of suffering is desire or hunger. As we will be talking some more about this truth, it would be as well to quote the text in full.

> What now, Brothers, is the Noble Truth of the Origin of Suffering? It is that Craving which gives rise to fresh rebirth, and bound by greed for pleasure, now here now there, finds ever fresh delight. It is the Sensual craving, the Craving for Individual existence, the Craving for Eternity.

The Root of Desire

A Zen master said do not worry about the leaves, flowers, and branches; go for the root. It is like having a big weed in the garden. While one cuts away at the flowers or leaves or even the main stem, the weed will always flourish again. But if one cuts out the root, then of themselves the flowers, leaves, and stem will wither and die. So many worry about the leaves and flowers, worry about how they behave, whether they think good thoughts or not, whether they are loving or compassionate. Constantly they try to purify their minds and behavior. But, alas, rarely do they go for the root.

Therefore, all this pruning and cutting back are largely wasted. For a time the garden looks good: clean and neat. But come the moment when the pruning slackens, through illness, fatigue, inattention, or difficult times, out comes the weed again in full bloom. The root is hard and tough. It is so deeply entrenched one often despairs at the very idea of cutting it out. This root is the "craving for individual existence"; the craving to be "someone"—someone with an identity, someone important. In sum, it is *the craving to be unique, not just while we live, but eternally.*

One of the countless ways this craving shows itself is through what we call nationalism. The Israelites saw themselves as the chosen race, the Germans as the Master race. When I was a child in Britain, we used to sing a song that went, "When Britain first at heaven's command / Arose from out the azure main." The Japanese traditionally saw themselves as descended from the Sun God and their Emperor as his incarnation; for the Chinese, everyone outside their land was a barbarian.

In 1957 the world was startled by a small round object circling the earth going beep! beep! It was immediately dubbed Sputnik by the Americans, but, despite the humor in the name, this small object, no bigger than a grapefruit, threw the United States into a flurry of activity. They were no longer number one in technology. So the race began to be first in space.

Who does not want to be first, to be the best, to be outstanding, head and shoulders above the crowd? A book on management was the rage a short while ago and most probably it was its title, *In Search of Excellence*, more than anything else that made it a best-seller. To excel. To be the one. That is the root: diplomas, titles, medals, ranks, grades, and classes all feed it. Competition is not an instinct: it is the natural result of the need for *individual* existence, the need to be unique. It is what underlies the famous struggle to survive. Wars, international, civil, domestic, are fought in its name. It is the power behind politics and sport, behind business, even behind the arts and sciences. For each one, what is good is that which supports individual existence. What is bad is what is opposed, antagonistic to it. Each will cooperate with whatever sustains it and will fight whatever damages. This lust for individuality is like a raging fire.

Idolatry

Out of ignorance I choose a part of the whole and idolize it while turning my back on the rest. Idolatry is just this: to take a part and treat it as though it were the whole. It is possible only when I ignore the rest, all that is not it. However, the whole is forever wanting to reclaim the part and reintegrate it. We resist this integration, which we perceive as aggression, by building up walls of prejudice and rejection, choosing this as good and that as bad; this as right and that as wrong; this as acceptable, that as unacceptable. Because we have chosen a part as the whole, we have now to nourish it, and we do so at the expense of the whole. This is possible through *greed*. And against the encroachment of the whole that we see as the other, the enemy, we become *aggressive*. Ignorance, greed, and aggression are the unholy alliance on which "I am something" is based.

"I am something" is to be distinct and separate and, we claim, absolute. To be distinct and absolute is to be unique. But buried in this claim is a profound contradiction. What is distinct is always a part and can never be the whole; indeed, to be separate is to be a part. What is absolute can only be the whole and can never be broken into parts, can never be separated. The search to be the absolute is the search to be the one; but our claim is to be the one in a particular, separate, and distinct form. In this absolute-but-distinct-one lies the contradiction. Because of this contradiction we are doomed to chase an impossible dream. The Holy Grail, the promised land, the philosopher's stone, Shambhala, Shangri La, can never be got in experience, but we cannot resist the seduction of the siren's call, and so daily we go out in search and daily we are frustrated and disappointed. A new job, a new house, a new car, a new lover, a new _____.

Anyone who has children knows the conflict that rages constantly as they clamor for attention. "Look at me! I am the only one!" It is called sibling rivalry. Invariably also, in a family, antagonism exists between father and son, and mother and daughter, to which Freud gave the names Oedipus complex and Electra complex. He said these have sexual origins, with the son wanting to displace the father in the mother's affections, and the daughter to displace the mother in the father's. This may be so, but the reason for the antagonism is simpler and more direct than psychoanalysts would have us believe. To the extent there is an Oedipus complex, the son wants to be the only one and he sees the father as an obstruction to this end. The father too wants to be the only one, and sees the son as a growing menace. A similar tension exists between mother and daughter. But we cannot remove this will-to-be-the-only-one by analysis or counseling.

As well as the conflict that occurs in family life, there are the politics of the office, of the club, of the group, to say nothing of the state and of the nation. These politics are the tussle and struggle to impress, to dominate, to attract, to be the one, to be absolute and distinct.

This is not meant as an indictment of the human race. What is best as well as what is worst grows out of this thrust to be absolute and distinct. It is, furthermore, not only in the human being this thrust exists. If you have seen two cats staring at each other, two dogs sniffing at each other, two rams butting heads, two deer locking horns, you have seen this effort to be separate, to be distinct, to be the only one. It is called the struggle for survival. Some biologists go so far as to say that all life organisms are simply carriers of genes, and it is to the genes' struggle to be the one that we owe the drama of life. This theory comes from a study called sociobiology and has triggered much discussion among biologists, some holding strongly to the view, others questioning it.

At first this sounds depressing and pessimistic, but from a closer view we see it is not. We must remember the drama is played out against the background of wholeness; wholeness that is beyond all conception, that is peace that passes all understanding. Self-luminous, without limit or restriction, the repository of all beauty and truth, it is our true nature. Individual, distinct existence, called I or me, is the son or daughter of this true nature.

Zen has a saying: "The thief my son!" (or "The thief my daughter!"). That which is most precious is a thief. This reflects the inner contradiction of the claim to be absolute and distinct. "I" is that which, at one and the same time, is the most precious and also a thief. Each time we say "I" or "me" or "it is mine" this contradiction is expressed. Sensitive people are aware of the contradiction as a pervasive sense of shame, a feeling of being a phony, or sometimes even the feeling of depersonalization, of not existing at all.

This inner contradiction nevertheless has a basis in truth: I *am* absolute *and at the same time* distinct, but each in a different way. As a self-luminous, true nature I am absolute; as "I" or "me" I am distinct.

An Analogy

Let us try to make this more accessible. Suppose you are holding a mirror in your hand and looking at the sun reflected in it. What you see is the sun; it is not the moon or the headlights of a car, nor is it a candle; it is the sun. Nonetheless, it is not so, because it is a *reflection*, and as such it is not reality, not that which is reflected. It is not the sun. But then, as a reflection, it does have reality, reality borrowed from the light of the sun to be sure, but nonetheless real. To understand the last sentence one should remember a dream is a dream, it is not reality; but even so as a dream it is real. When you say, "I had a dream last night," you are talking about the dream as something real.

So it is with "I." "I" is real in so far as it is the reflection of true nature, and as true nature it is *absolute*, whole, one. But, then, "I" is not real; it is a reflection of this true nature. But as a reflection it is real, though it borrows this reality from true nature. Moreover, as specific reflection it is *distinct*.

A disciple of a Hindu teacher said that all was an illusion. The teacher said, "Do not insult Brahman!"

Narcissus and the Zen Master

Another myth will help us to understand this, particularly when we juxtapose it to a Zen story. It is the myth of Narcissus.

Narcissus was a handsome youth who happened to see his reflection in the surface of a pool. He became so enamored of himself that he tried to embrace himself, fell into the pool, and drowned.

Like Narcissus, our true nature sees itself reflected, reflected in the mirror of being. However, forgetting that "I" is a reflection, it takes what is distinct to be absolute. In other words, we try to embrace our true nature within the confines of experience, and so drown in illusion.

A Zen master came to awakening while crossing a river. He saw himself reflected in the water and at that moment awakening burst upon him. He wrote a poem that said:

> I meet him wherever I go
> He is the same as me
> Yet I am not him!
> Only if you understand
> Will you identify with what you are.[1]

Whereas the reflection is the reflection of the sun (he is the same as me), even so the sun itself is not the reflection (yet I am not him). It is our believing that the sun *is* the reflection

---

1   Attributed to Zen Master Liang-chieh, from Chang Chung-Yuan, *Original Teaching of Ch'an Buddhism* (New York: Vintage Books, 1971), p. 60.

that leads us to believe the ego is both absolute and distinct. In the myth this is symbolized by Narcissus embracing his reflection.

A Sufi poem by Attar is also pertinent to what we are saying:

> The Sun of my Perfection is a Glass
> Wherein from Seeing into Being pass
> All who, reflecting as reflected see
> Themselves in Me, Me in Them; not Me,
> But all of Me that a contracted Eye is comprehensive
> of Infinity:
>
> ....
>
> All that you have been, and seen, and done, and thought,
> Not You but I, have seen, and been, and wrought:
> I was the sin which from Myself rebelled;
> I was the Remorse that toward myself compelled;
> I was the teacher who led the track;
> I was the friend who pulled you back;
> Sin and contrition—Retribution owed
> And canceled—Pilgrim, Pilgrimage and Road,
> Was but myself toward Myself; and your
> Arrival but Myself at my own door;
> Who in your fraction of Myself, behold
> Myself within the mirror Myself hold
> To see Myself in, and each part of Me
> That sees herself, though drowned, shall ever see.
> Come, you lost atoms, to your Centre draw,
> And be the Eternal Mirror that you saw;
> Rays that have wandered into darkness wide,
> Return, and back into your Sun subside.[2]

To this reality-illusion we have given the name ego.

When we think of ego we always think of something undesirable, something to be got rid of. However, in a true spiritual

---

2   A. J. Arberry, *Sufism: An Account of the Mysteries of Islam* (New York: Harper Torchbooks), p. 109.

practice one does not try to change or get rid of anything. The effort to do so implies the very judgment of good and bad, which, as we said, is at the foundation of the problem. The reflection has its place, as does the sun; the ego has its place, as does what we have been calling true nature.

Reflection and Reality

When we see a red hat it is not, scientists tell us, a red hat that we see. What happens is the light from the sun falls on the hat and is mostly absorbed by it. However, not all the light is absorbed. The light that is not absorbed is reflected from the hat as color, in this example, red. What we see is what the hat is not. However, this does not mean to say what we see is not valid. It merely means what we thought was the case turns out to be something different when we look more closely. Nor does it mean we should change our way of looking or even stop saying the hat is red. What it does mean is we should be prepared to look more closely.

Dirt has been said to be matter in the wrong place, and in a similar way one could say that error is truth that has not been examined closely enough, and so therefore is perceived wrongly.

Hindu teachers of the spiritual way love to tell the story of the man who saw a snake on the path leading from his house. He was terrified because he felt if he went outside the snake would bite him. So he waited in the house for the snake to go away. One day passed and another, and still the snake lay there, coiled up. A neighbor became concerned because he had not seen the man around for sometime, and called on him to be sure he was all right. "How did you get here?" gasped the man. "Did you not see the snake on the pathway?" The neighbor realized what was the trouble and said, "Come with me, I will show you." They went together to examine the viper more closely. As they drew near the man let out a sigh of relief. It was not a snake, it was a coil of rope. At that moment all the tension and fear that came from not having looked more closely dropped away.

Spiritual practice, particularly meditative practice, is precisely this looking more closely. When one meditates on the question "Who am I?", one looks closely at "I" and realizes that what one thought to be real is a reflection. The illusion that the reflection is indeed real comes from ignorance, which, as we have said, is the power behind illusion. Ignorance is turning away from true nature. When through meditation we look more closely, we no longer turn away, ignorance loses its power, and so the illusion that reflection is reality drops away. The man in an instant was aware of his error. At one moment it was a snake, at the next it was a coil of rope. In the same way spiritual awakening, or no longer turning away from it, happens in an instant.

The ego is not something bad, it is not of the devil, and we will not have to burn in hell because of it, nor is the suffering we experience in life a punishment for the sin of "I." Inherent in ego is a contradiction, and it is from this contradiction that our suffering comes, and also the suffering we inflict on others. Because of this contradiction we are forever restless, forever on the way to some resolution that in its turn is forever eluding us.

Summing Up

Let us sum up again. To be simultaneously absolute and distinct is contradictory. The absolute is beyond form. As Buddha said in a quotation we gave earlier, our true nature "is unborn, unbecome, unmade, unconditioned." To be distinct, on the other hand, means to be a form separated from all others; it means to be the unique center of all that is.

This contradiction pervades our whole conscious life, and the next few chapters will go more deeply into some of the implications of this. Then we will be able to understand more clearly what Buddha meant when he said that suffering is the basis of existence, the mortar that binds together the bricks of experience, and also why a spiritual life is necessary.

Chapter 4
The Spectrum of Thought

People who hear about Zen often think it would be difficult for the Westerner to practice because it comes from the Orient where there is such a different way of thought. This is not so. Buddhism first came into being in India and was developed in Asia, yet it has universal value, and a Westerner, no less than a Chinese or Japanese, can practice Zen and come to deep awakening. Nor is it only the Westerner who has to struggle. Many Eastern masters work for a long time before coming to awakening, and many stories exist to attest to that fact. For example, Ananda, who was Buddha's assistant, worked for twenty-five years and still had not awakened even at Buddha's death. It was, incidentally, because of Ananda that we have the sutras of Buddhism. He had such a prodigious memory he could repeat and has transcribed Buddha's teachings word for word. But despite his memory, despite his great mental agility, maybe because of it, he still had a hard time.

A Zen master whose name was Kyogen also practiced for a long time and eventually became so dispirited he gave it up. He spent his time instead caring for the graves of deceased monks and masters in a nearby cemetery. Then one day a pebble struck against the broom he was using to sweep the pathway, and at that moment he came to deep awakening.

Yet another master, Mumon, compiled a collection of koans, which have become very famous and are still used today. It is called the *Mumonkan,* and we use it, among other collections, at the Montreal Zen Centre. Mumon struggled for eight years before he came to awakening.

Zen master Dogen, the founder of the Japanese Soto Zen school, was haunted by a problem, one that may trouble you, too: If it is true we are whole and complete, why is it that all the Buddhas and patriarchs had to work so hard to awaken? Dogen began to practice Zen because of this question, the practice that ultimately led to his great awakening. He put it this way, "If it is true I am whole and complete, why do I have to work so hard to know this for myself?"

In Genesis it is said:

> So He drove out the man; and He placed at the east of the garden of Eden the Cherubim, and the flame of the sword which turned every way, to keep the way of the tree of life.[1]

What then is this flaming sword that bars the way to wholeness, to our true nature?

The Human Fault

The answer given in Zen is that it is the tyranny of thought that bars the way. For example, Chinese Zen master Ta Hui said:

> Conceptualization is a deadly hindrance, more injurious than poisonous snakes or fierce beasts. Brilliant and intellectual persons always abide in the cave of conceptualization; they can never get away from it in all their activities.[2]

---

1 Gen. 3:24-25.

2 Chang Chen-chi, *The Practice of Zen* (London: Rider & Co., 1960), p. 71.

Another master, Huang Po, said:

> If you can only rid yourselves of conceptual thought you
> will have accomplished everything. But if you do not rid
> yourselves of conceptual thought in a flash even though you
> strive for an eternity you will never accomplish anything.
> Enmeshed in meritorious practices you will be unable to
> attain Awakening.[3]

By "ridding yourself of conceptual thought" Huang Po did
not mean one should make the mind blank. This is a very common
mistake made by people who come to practice Zen or other kinds
of meditation. The reasoning they follow on the way to this mistake
is, Our problem is conceptual thought; the solution therefore is
to stop thinking. But to make the mind a blank simply deadens
the mind and is of no avail.

This is a most critical point, and to understand fully what
Ta Hui meant by saying that conceptualization is more injurious
than poisonous snakes or fierce beasts, and what Huang Po meant
by ridding oneself of conceptual thought, we have to understand
the part that that kind of thinking plays in our life. To do this
we must put thought into perspective and understand its place
in consciousness. Most people believe that thinking is simply a
way of solving problems, but although solving problems is one
of its functions, it is by no means the only one. It is obvious
also that Huang Po means much more by conceptual thought
than solving problems; as he says, it enmeshes one in "meritorious
practices."

---

3   John Blofield, trans., *The Zen Teachings of Huang Po* (London: The Buddhist
Society, 1958), p. 31.

A Word of Caution

Do you remember the story about the man who lost his key and persisted in looking for it under the light instead of in the bushes where it could be found, but where also, alas, it was very dark? So far our explanation of the human situation has been quite simple, although—and we must make the distinction—not necessarily easy. The next few chapters may seem a little more complex, because we have to go into the bushes.

Thought as the Wounded Surgeon

What we can say at this stage is that, as we have seen, we are wounded in our innermost being; our conscious life has a fault running through it. We are divided against ourselves. This division, dualism, *dukkha*,[4] call it what you will, lies at the root of conscious life. And, not only this, it lies at the root of suffering also. Thinking is the way that, as human beings, we try to heal the wound and restore wholeness. Though it is abortive, yet we return to it again and again as a way out of our difficulties. We live forever in the hope of eternal rest, of an end to the stress and tension of life, all the while clinging tenaciously to that which perpetuates this stress, all the while clinging tenaciously to thought, the wounded surgeon.

The Spectrum in Detail

Just as white light projected through a prism displays itself as a spectrum of color, so true nature projected through the prism of separation shows itself as a spectrum of thought, from ambiguity to dream. We want to describe some of this spectrum, and then

---

4   A Sanskrit word meaning duality and suffering. See Albert Low, *Iron Cow of Zen* (Boston: Charles E. Tuttle, 1991), p. 121.

in the next few chapters we will delve more deeply into the origin of the inner contradiction that makes thought necessary and brings the spectrum into being.

During the discussion in this chapter, to make it easier, we can simply state the contradiction as between yes and/or no, but remember that yes/no also means good/bad, right/wrong, me/you, and all the other opposites in thought.

Now let us go back again to what Huang Po said and try to understand his meaning. What is "conceptual thought"? Furthermore what does he mean when he says, "Enmeshed in *meritorious* practices you will be unable to attain Awakening." One might well ask, "Is it not through meritorious practices, through doing good, that we progress along the spiritual path?" Certainly, as the story we told at the beginning of the book showed, Emperor Wu thought that way, and so do many others. Yet, as we pointed out with the story of Adam and Eve, discriminating good from bad somehow lies at the root of our trouble. So we must also understand what Huang Po means by *meritorious practices*.

We said there is not simply one way of thinking but many, and they can be made into a scale.

nonreflected awareness	*beyond* YES and NO
ambiguity	YES as NO
creative thinking	YES and NO
	happily married
dilemma	both YES and NO, but neither YES nor NO
worry	cannot resolve YES and NO
moral thinking	assert YES over NO or NO over YES
ON/OFF thinking	YES or NO
more or less thinking	from YES to NO
inner monologue	neither YES nor NO
dream	YES and NO interchangeable
sleep	YES and NO absent

Awareness and Sleep

At the top of the scale is *nonreflected awareness*. As you may remember, we spoke at the beginning of the book about a knowing that is so complete, so without limit, that we can refer to it only as *not knowing* (in Japanese it is *mu-shin*, "no mind"). We also called it bodhi. The words bodhi and Buddha are from the same verb root and both refer in different ways to our true nature. Our true nature is nonreflected awareness, awareness that is not even limited by itself. There is not some *thing* that is aware, no spirit or soul, no ego or self. Awareness is its own being. This is good news, as it means we do not have *to be something* to be aware, let alone be something special. We do not have to be a brain, or a body, or a realized self, or a developed self to be aware.

Nor, on the other hand, do we have to be aware *of something* to be. We do not have to experience *anything* to be. This implies of course that we do not have to have some particular belief or creed, we do not have to belong to this or that religious group. Awareness is being and this is Buddha. As a Zen master said, "From the beginning all beings are Buddha." Also since being is aware it means the world is not dead, cold, and abstract, but alive and intelligent. A Buddhist scripture says that awareness is being, being is awareness. Or more technically, "emptiness is form, form is emptiness."

But this emptiness (in Japanese, *ku*, in Sanskrit, *shunyata*), as Zen master Yasutani roshi said,

> is not mere emptiness. It is that which is living, dynamic, devoid of mass, unfixed, beyond individuality or personality the matrix of all phenomena. Here we have the fundamental principle of Buddhism.[5]

---

5   P. Kapleau, ed., *The Three Pillars of Zen* (New York: John Weatherhill, 1966), p. 74.

Do you remember Bodhidharma's words: "Vast emptiness and not a thing that can be called holy"? It is this we are calling nonreflected awareness, and what Yasutani called *ku*.

Nonreflected awareness has its counterpart in deep sleep. Most of us think that we lose awareness during sleep. However, although it is true we lose *consciousness*, we do not lose awareness because we *are* awareness, or maybe it would be better to say, Buddha nature is awareness. A mother can sleep through all kinds of noise, yet let her young baby but whimper and she is alert in an instant. A sleepwalker can walk unerringly even through difficult and dangerous surroundings. Many surgeons have come to realize that although patients may be anaesthetized they are still aware. More than this, numerous accounts have been given by people who, even though declared clinically dead, after resuscitation, said they were aware the whole time.

However, the awareness that is sleep is the awareness of *nothing*. To put this in words with which we are familiar, in sleep we ignore all. Research on sleep has shown it is not a simple, passive condition, but is its own form of activity. In one way there is no difference between sleep and nonreflected awareness, since both are encounters with wholeness. In another way they are quite different.

Because it might make what we have to say easier to understand, we will continue with a description of the levels of thinking with a discussion of on/off thinking, leaving aside for the present the inner monologue and dreaming. We will then work our way up the scale to discuss ambiguity. On/off thinking is what we use to solve our technical problems and is therefore the type of thought that we are most familiar with, so it makes a natural entrance point.

On/Off Thinking

As we know, the fastest-growing industry in the world at the moment is the electronics industry. This growth is particularly evident in the home entertainment field and in computers. The feature that underlies this development is a very simple way of thinking called *binary logic.*

Binary logic, or if you prefer, binary thinking, is the simplest way we have of thinking, but even highly complex technology comes out of it, including compact disc recordings, photographs of Jupiter and Mars taken from satellite rockets, complex medical diagnostic equipment and so on. Even so, binary logic is just the logic of the light switch that is either on or off.

Before the computer was developed there used to be what were called *Hollerith machines.* Cards that had been previously punched with holes were passed through these machines. As each card passed through, a switch would be held in an off position by the card until a hole appeared. The switch would make contact and, for that moment, the machine would be on. A counter tallied the number of times the switch was on and off.

The same on/off logic is the logic of the computer. The fact that with its help we can reproduce music and pictures, we can count and calculate, as well as simulate some of our thinking, shows to what a great extent our minds are influenced by this logic.

This type of thinking is normally called logical thinking, or either/or thinking. According to it, everything is either one thing or another, either black or white, right or wrong, male or female, young or old, possible or not possible, and so on. There is something comforting about it. We have the feeling of certainty because of it, and engineers and scientists depend on it. A measurement is either right or wrong, and millions of lives could well depend on whether it is right or wrong. Through technology this type of thinking has come to have an enormous influence on our lives, so much so that many claim it to be the only correct kind of thinking, and other ways are wrong, or at least inferior.

More or Less Thinking

Not all light switches are of the on/off variety. There are also dimmer switches in which the light is more or less on or off.

This switch allows one to pass through an infinity of more or less, from barely on to fully on. On occasions the mind also thinks in this way. For example, if someone were to ask whether you are going out tonight you could well answer possibly or probably. Both appear somewhere along a yes/no spectrum with possibly being nearer no and probably nearer yes. This location moreover is flexible, possibly easily turning into probably and vice versa depending on the circumstances. This type of thinking too has been simulated by computers in what are called neurological networks or fields. So that we can refer to it again later, let us call it *more or less* thinking.

Ought Thinking

Another kind of thinking is one we will call ought thinking: I *ought* to do this, I *must* do that, I *should* do something else, and so on. Another name could be *morality* thinking, thinking that asserts good over bad. However, anticipating what we will deal with in greater depth later, we should make a distinction between *moral* thinking and *ethical* thinking. Moral thinking is based on fixed rules called moral codes that are given in terms of black or white, "thou shalt" and "thou shalt not." Ethical conduct, on the other hand, is thinking that is sensitive to the nuances of the situation, and this sensitivity comes out of a high tolerance for ambiguity and a keen awareness of wholeness and unity. When Huang Po spoke about being enmeshed in meritorious practices, he meant practices based on ought thinking.

Worrying

Worrying is accompanied by feelings of confusion, uncertainty, anxiety, and indecisiveness. Whereas on/off thinking is certain and clear cut, and more or less thinking smooth and flexible, worry is neither the one nor the other since it is neither clear nor flexible. Or, one could also say it is *both* on/off *and* more or less thinking, since it has the rigidity of the former and the uncertainty of the latter.

Dilemma

With a dilemma there are at least two, although sometimes more, ways of acting in response to a situation. Although both ways are equally good or desirable (or both equally bad and undesirable), only one can be selected and acted on at any given moment. In other words, at some particular time *to do the right thing is to do the wrong thing, which is to reject the right thing.*

This may sound somewhat heavy, so let me give you a couple of examples and you will recognize in a moment what is meant.

Should a woman have an abortion if and when she wishes? We can say, "Yes! It is her body and no one has the right to dictate what she should or should not do with her body." As we know, many people hold to this point of view with passion. Or we can say, "No! Because she would be destroying life, and thou shalt not kill is an imperative that has been acknowledged by the great religions." Again, as we know, many people hold to this with equal passion.

However, for some people these two alternatives have equal weight. Therefore for them to do the right thing, in this instance to allow the woman to do as she will with her body, is to do the wrong thing, which is to stand back while life is destroyed. The opposite is also true. If we prevent a woman from having an abortion, which is now considered the right thing, some arbitrary power would be decreeing what she should do with her body, which many people would say is a wrong thing.

Another example: Should the government promote public transport and restrict the use of private vehicles, or should the government allow market forces to determine whether public transport or private vehicles should be used? One might say, "Yes! The government should promote public transport, and unless it does so the carbon dioxide emissions will so pollute the atmosphere that dire consequences are in store for our children

44

and grandchildren." Or one might say, "No! By doing so the government would completely disrupt the economy, which is so dependent on the automotive industry."

These examples are like the story of a judge who having heard the counsel for the defense, turned to him and said, "Yes! You are right!" Then the counsel for the prosecution stood and said his piece. Again the judge turned to him and said, "Yes! You are right!" Then the clerk of the court, hot under the collar, leapt up and exclaimed, "But, m'lud, they both can't be right." And the judge turned to him and said, "Yes! You are right!"

On/off thinking demands a yes or no: yes, a woman should be the one to decide to carry the baby, *or* no, she does not have this right; yes, the government should promote public transport, no, the government should not do so. Dilemma thinking says one *cannot* say yes or no, because both are right, or both are wrong. However, and this is essential to a dilemma because it distinguishes it from ambiguity, one has to give an answer. Not to act is itself a decision. One must find an answer; one must make a decision. One *cannot* say yes or no, but one *must* say yes or no.

Worry is a hybrid thought bred from on/off and dilemma thinking. On/off demands one alternative, whereas dilemma thinking keeps coming up with two. And so worry just goes back and forth, from one horn of the dilemma to the other and back. Worry is similar to more or less thinking, but different since it cannot rest, but is always on the move. "If I allow my daughter to continue to go out with the crowd she is with, she'll land in trouble. But on the other hand, if I don't let her choose her own friends, how will she ever stand on her own feet?" If you are a parent this will surely sound familiar to you.

Ought thinking, like worry, is also a hybrid; but with this thinking, instead of worrying about the problem and constantly going back and forth between the two alternatives, we simply refuse to entertain one or the other of them. "No, she cannot go out with that crowd because it is wrong!" We make this refusal even though the dilemma keeps demanding we do entertain both alternatives. The rejected or ignored one does not go away. It keeps pressing for its own resolution. The need to overcome this pressure accounts for the force many people require to back up moral thinking, and to contain the potentially explosive situation that this creates.

Creative Thinking

We have yet two more ways of thinking to consider. First there is the way we could call *creative* thinking. This is a legitimate resolution of the dilemma and is the way to get harmony between two points of view that are interdependent but which exclude one another. Again let me give you an example.

People who used a certain very high building complained because the elevators were too slow. To install more or faster elevators would have been very costly; however, the owners had to do something because having to wait would make people avoid the building, which would mean loss of custom and so on. So what should the owners do? Some bright person said, "Give the people something interesting to do while they wait." But what? Then another came up with the solution: install mirrors. Everyone likes looking at themselves in a mirror, as well as at other people looking at themselves. By installing mirrors the tedium of waiting could be overcome with the least cost.

Ambiguity

You will have gathered by now that the word "thinking" has been used in a very loose way. We have been meaning a way of using the mind, or *a way the mind functions*. For now we will continue to use the word in this way, but in the next chapter we will use "awareness" in its place. For the moment though, let us not get caught up in this distinction.

Although everyone knows about ambiguity, its importance in our conscious life is often overlooked, except in the realm of the arts. Poetry, music, architecture, painting, really all the arts, when they are authentic, have ambiguity as a basic ingredient. Beethoven said music is a higher revelation than science. Insofar as the spirit of music dwells in ambiguity and that of science dwells in either/or thinking, Beethoven was right. Ambiguity is also, as we will see, at the basis of mystical and spiritual life.

The following is an example of poetic thought from T. S. Eliot's *The Waste Land*:

> The river's tent is broken: the last fingers of leaf
> Clutch and sink into the wet bank. The wind
> crosses the brown land, unheard. The nymphs have
>   departed.[6]

The imagery in these lines is both evocative and ambiguous. "The river's tent" is the canopy of leaves and branches that arch over the river. There is an ambiguity in the tent's being "broken." "Breaking camp" means to go, to depart; but the phrase can also mean the tent is destroyed. "The river's tent is broken" suggests it is autumn. But it could also imply some violence has broken the leaves and branches, and, by implication, the idyllic life. Or it could imply both.

Eliot's poem is haunted by the death of the sacred, by barrenness, and by the break-up of meaning. This image of a broken camp contributes to this feeling, as does "The nymphs have departed." Nymphs are spiritual forces of beauty and sublimity. Or are they nymphomaniacs, women who have an insatiable desire for sex regardless of with whom, where, or how? The clash of meaning coming out of this particular ambiguity, right next to "The river's tent is broken," with its ambiguity of whether the

---

6   T. S. Eliot, "The Waste Land," *Collected Works 1909-1935* (London: Faber & Faber, 1936), p. 68.

nymphs left of their own accord or were driven out, adds to the potential horror of the setting, or its potential beauty.

With such a brief analysis we can hardly touch the richness of the poetry and can only hint at its potential. But it does show that when reading a poem one constantly has to dwell in that domain in which there is no certainty, or rather, where alternative certainties intermingle and contrast, building up struggle, tension, and resolution. This is the domain of ambiguity, and it is on its inherent tension and resolution that much of poetry is built.

In the scale that appears on page 39 ambiguity is put at the top. This is because all other kinds of thinking are derived from it. It is the first departure of sentience from Buddha nature. We will be returning to this ambiguity repeatedly and will find it has many different guises. One of the things we want to show is that ambiguity is common to all life, or that life comes from the urge to find some resolution of it. Right now we want to stress that our conscious life is based on ambiguity, and therefore that a spiritual life must take it into consideration.

Some Examples of Ambiguity

Ambi means "two," as we can see in such words as ambidextrous (able to use both hands equally well), ambivalent (to be of two minds), and ambivert (tending in two directions). Ambiguity is frequently used instead of vagueness, but we will be using it only to mean that there are two equally satisfactory ways of viewing a situation, *but one can choose only one at any particular time.*

A question often asked at workshops is, "Where do Yin and Yang fit in with an understanding of Zen?" Anyone familiar with New Age literature knows that the Yin-Yang symbol appears very often in books and articles. Nowadays it is almost a requirement that New Age writings make some reference to it.

If we can spend just a few minutes reflecting on Yin-Yang, we will not only gain a deeper understanding of the implications of ambiguity, but will also gain some understanding of why Yin-Yang is so attractive.

The standard symbol for Yin and Yang is as follows:

Yin is feminine, passive; Yang is masculine and active. Swiss psychologist C. G. Jung wrote that the psychological make-up of a woman contains a masculine component that he called the *animus*, and a man's make-up contains a feminine component, the *anima*. The above symbol retains the same idea with its two little circles: the white circle in the black sphere and the black circle in the white. This implies that in Yin there is always Yang; in Yang there is always Yin. This is the ultimate in ambiguity.

Yin and Yang arise out of Tao. Tao can be understood in many different ways, but for our purposes it can be called Wholeness, Oneness, or Unity. Some people therefore draw the symbol with an outer circle depicting the Tao, implying that Tao is the One out of which Yin and Yang emerge:

This outer circle, however, is a mistake, and showing why will help us to make a very important point about the basic ambiguity underlying our conscious life.

Ambiguity is quite unlike *duality*, which implies that there are two separate things; it is different from *polarity* in which the two are polar opposites (for example, the north and south pole of a magnet); it is also different from *complementary* in which the one is interdependent with the other, for example, a nut and a bolt. In ambiguity the one *is* the other, while *at the same time it is separate from it*.

Let me give another well-known example, this time a Western one:

In this picture the outline is ambiguous, it being the head of both a young and an old woman. The outline of the young woman exactly matches the outline of the old woman: when one is seen the other is absent, and vice versa. The illustration is therefore better in a way than the Yin-Yang symbol.

But returning to Yin and Yang for the moment, it is these that first emerge from unity, or Tao. On the scale that we gave above we showed this to be the case, and said that all ways of thought arise from ambiguity and that ambiguity in turn is the first departure from undifferentiated or nonreflected awareness. Because ambiguity is so close to unity, while also having affinities with duality, it is a very satisfying form of thinking. It is this satisfaction we feel when the ambiguity is expressed as Yin and Yang.

The Difference Between Ambiguity and Dilemma

Let us now look at why we said that the Western example is a better illustration of ambiguity and why this is so important. Please look at this picture and say what it is you see.

If I ask you, "Is it a vase or two faces?" how will you answer? "It is both?" "It is neither?" "It is a vase?" "It is two faces?" Suppose for the moment I say you *must* choose one way or another and, furthermore, let us say that if you choose correctly I will give you a wonderful prize. How can you choose "correctly"? One answer is as good as another. Neither has precedence. But, because I have said you must choose, now one *must* prevail over the other. But which one? This is a dilemma. You may come up with a creative solution, but if that is not possible, you are caught among the four different ways of responding. Until you are compelled, one way or another, to choose, there is simply an ambiguity. *When one is obliged to choose, an ambiguity becomes a dilemma.*

If you cannot come up with a creative solution to a dilemma but are under some compulsion to choose, you will begin to worry and grow anxious. You may even panic if the matter is important enough. You will slide constantly from one horn to the other and back. If the pressure continues to mount, you will be inclined to try to suppress one alternative or the other and become moralistic in defense of whichever you choose.

Another way out is to ignore one alternative completely. This is done by using on/off thinking. As we are becoming increasingly aware, logical, technical thought has had to overlook many alternative ways of action in the interests of the alternatives of efficiency and cost reduction. One result of this is pollution. But technological thinking does give us the possibility of action, which would probably be denied if we could not ignore part of experience.

Going back to the illustration of the vase and two faces, without the pressure to choose one way or the other, what you see is now a vase, now two faces. It is an ambiguity. It is like Yin and Yang: just as Yang implies Yin and Yin implies Yang, the vase implies the two faces and the two faces imply the vase. The outline for the one is the outline for the other. They are both independent yet at the same time they are interdependent. Independent, they are mutually exclusive: when you see the vase you do not see the two faces and vice versa. But each needs the other to be; they are mutually dependent.

Now one of the interesting things that comes up as one looks at this picture, and please verify this for yourself, is that the mind cannot rest for long on one alternative but has to ping-pong backward and forward between them. For example, if what you are seeing is the vase, after a while tension builds up in your mind until you switch over to seeing the two faces, and after a while you have to switch back to seeing the vase and so on. The switch, moreover, is not by a gradual transition from vase to faces but by a leap, a sudden transition from one to the other. Several scientists[7] have tried to find a reason for this having to go to and fro, and we take up the question in the next chapter. It will be an important part of what we will then be exploring.

Unity and the Scale of Thinking

Each level of thinking in the scale is, in its own way, a return to unity, a resolution of what we have called for the sake of simplicity the yes/no contradiction. Thinking comes from this need for *unity*. In the illustration of the faces and the vase each is a whole picture. The vase is a whole, the picture of the two faces is a whole. Each is, we could say, a unity, and that is why each has equal claim.

If one can accept this search for unity it becomes clear what worry and anxiety are about. We worry because we are constantly oscillating between alternative unities and *so, therefore, are paradoxically unable to find unity*. Because unity is not possible, pain and conflict result. The inner monologue, with which most people are familiar, is a complement to worry because it is an endeavor

---

7   Fred Attneave, "Multistability in Perception," *Scientific American* 225 (December 1971): 63.

to escape from the pain that this conflict causes. However, we have to leave further discussion of this particular point until later.

Unity as Identity

Another word that can be used instead of unity is "identity." Psychologist Erik Erikson was of the opinion that the search for identity is one of the essential dynamics of the human mind. Because of his writings we are all now familiar with the "identity crisis." A person with an identity crisis does not know who he or she is, and so worries a great deal. Someone in this condition is forever uncertain, anxious, and distressed. Identity crises are most likely to occur at times of transition in life, when going from one stage to another.

For example, going from being a teenager to being an adult is a period of transition when the person is now a child, now an adult, now back. An intolerable tension results and because of it teenagers can be so difficult to live with, erupting as they do into anger and tears for no apparent reason. For a child the primary need is for security; for an adult it is freedom to explore the world and to express oneself as an individual. It is the oscillation between these incompatible states and needs, from dependence to independence and back and the emergence of both of them simultaneously, that brings about the explosions in a teenager who inhabits both the world of the adult and the world of the child. Security and freedom are equally necessary, but they are so often incompatible.

On/off thinking also deals with identity. A law of identity was discovered by the Greek philosopher Aristotle. He expressed it in a very simple way by saying A = A, or, less technically, everything equals itself. Perhaps it might even be better to say everything *is* itself.

Some people might well find it surprising that anyone would go to the trouble of talking about such a law as this—everything equals itself, everything is itself. What the law is saying is so obvious: a chair is a chair; a pen is a pen; I am I; you are you;

A is A. It is all so obvious one would wonder why anyone would want to state it, let alone deny it. That everything is what it is is surely the root and anchor of our whole conscious life. How could it be otherwise?

Yet Buddhism does question it; it questions whether everything equals itself. The three basic laws in Buddhism are expressed as *no thing, no-self,* and *suffering.* We have been talking about suffering all along. We leave no-self until a bit later. Here we are talking about no thing. With the law of no thing Buddhism says an apple is not an apple, that is why it is called an apple. Another way of saying this is to say everything is impermanent, everything is change, nothing is itself even for an instant. It is because of this impermanence, the ceaseless flux of change that, to have a conscious life, we must use words and so pin down experience and immobilize it. Yet, ironically, it is precisely because we freeze experience in this way that it becomes so unsatisfactory.

At the beginning of this century there was a French philosopher, Henri Bergson, for whom also impermanence was a basic idea. A commentator on his philosophy summed up this part of Bergson's thinking as follows:

> Reality is flowing. This does not mean everything moves, changes and becomes; science and common experience tell us that. It means that movement, becoming, change is everything there is, there is nothing else. *There are no things that move and change and become; everything is movement, is change.*[8]

I have stressed the last part of the quotation to draw your attention to it.

Let us repeat. According to Aristotle and to Western tradition generally, everything is what it is. But Buddha, Bergson, and

---

8   H. Wilden Carr, ed., *Henri Bergson* (London: T. C. & E. C. Jack, 1911), p. 28.

others, including the philosopher Lucretius, all say there are no things, there is just the flow of change. It would seem common sense is on the side of things being what they are, but experience, which for some grows more bitter as the years pass, tells us otherwise. One has only to look in the mirror and then remember when that face did not have a single wrinkle or bags under the eyes, to realize the truth of impermanence. These two viewpointsthere are things and there are no thingsare incompatible, but neither can be rejected. That everything *is* requires no proof; but it is equally obvious, as Lucretius said, we cannot step into the same river twice. There is no more or less between these two, no gradient, just as there is no more or less between the vase and the two faces. But, similarly, neither can be rejected in favor of the other.

Ambiguity and Creativity

The dilemma therefore underlies all of our conscious life, all of our action. The stress of life, the difficulties, all come because in the interest of unity, in the interest of what we are, we have to choose but cannot choose. This cuts right through all we do and all we think. One way of escape is to turn the dilemmas into problems. We do this by having projects and goals. Thus, for example, the adolescent, torn between the two needs of security and freedom, could plan on going to a university and believe that in this would lie the resolution of his or her dilemma. This plan would set up a number of problems, such as what subjects to take, how to finance, which university to attend, and so on, all of which could mask the fundamental dilemma. This is just a temporary solution, a Band Aid on the wound, because, despite appearances, the dilemma persists. Another way out is spiritual work. Both creative thinking and spiritual work are possible only when we can tolerate the dilemma and have suspended on/off and more or less thinking, which we normally use to solve problems in life. It is for this reason that spiritual and creative activity are both hard work.

To give an idea of what is meant by tolerating the dilemma, let me remind you of a story that every school child must know. It concerns a man named Archimedes. The king of the country in which Archimedes lived received a beautiful golden crown as a gift. Being somewhat greedy, he wanted to know how much gold there was in the crown. He summoned Archimedes and ordered him to determine this. Now the easiest thing to have done would have been to melt the crown down into a cube of gold, measure the height, breadth, and length, multiply them together, and arrive at the answer. To do this would have been to destroy the crown. So what was Archimedes to do? To preserve the crown, he couldn't melt it down; to know the amount of gold, it seemed he had to melt it down. It was a bit like the problem I gave earlier. Choose the right picture and you will get a prize, although here it was find the right answer or you'll lose your head.

Archimedes must have walked around with this dilemma for quite a while. Time would have been passing and he would have had to come up with some way out. Then one day he got into his bath and lo and behold the resolution fell on him like a ton of bricks and he leapt out of his bath and ran down the street yelling "Eureka! I've found it!" What had he found? As he lowered himself into the bath the water rose up along the side of the tub by a corresponding amount. He realized the water displaced was equal to the volume of his body. All he had to do was to put the crown in a bowl of water and measure the amount of water it displaced.

Only by tolerating the tension of the dilemma, by not taking one or the other alternatives originally offered, was Archimedes able to come to this insight. In the words we have been using, it is only by suspending on/off thinking that he could do this.

To suspend thinking in this way means one has to go into the bushes, that is, one has to pass through worry, uncertainty, and anxiety. As we have said, it also means we have to suspend morality thinking. As long as we think we know what is good and bad, right and wrong, we cannot enter into creative, or meditative, thinking. In the words of Jesus:

> Truly, truly I say to you unless a grain of wheat falls to earth and dies it remains alone; but if it dies it bears much fruit. He who loves his life loses it, he who hates his life in this world will keep it for eternal life.[9]

We have to let go of all we cling to most desperately, and what most of us cling to is the belief we know what is right and good, not only for ourselves but for all.

The question might well have arisen in the reader's mind, "But how are we to suspend this type of thinking? How are we to let go of the belief that we can sort it all out?" To try to answer this we must penetrate a little more deeply into what it means to be human, and to do this we need a new chapter.

---

9   St. John, 12:24-25.

Chapter 5
Oneness

The Many Faces of One

The philosopher Plotinus said, "It is by the One that all beings are beings. If not a One a thing is not. No army, no choir, no flock exists except that it be One. No house nor even ship except that it exists as the One."[1]

Has it ever occurred to you that everything we see is one: one table, one pen, one piece of paper? This one is made more obvious in the French language in which the speaker does not say "a pen" but "one pen": *une plume. Une plume* means both "one pen" and "a pen." We speak about "a" room even though it has chairs, tables, ornaments, and so on. We also talk about a city, a world, a life. It is always *one.* However, we do not only see one, we also think one. The word *comprehend* means "to hold together in the mind." Understanding is the attempt to bring together experience into *one comprehensive whole.* Furthermore, all our art forms have unity as a natural basis. A picture, building,

---

1   Elmer O'Brien, *The Essential Plotinus* (New York: New American Library, Mentor Books, 1964), pp. 80-81.

piece of music, piece of sculpture, play, or story must be a unity. In dramatic art this has been formalized in the three unities of time, place, and action.

The need for unity is also well known by interrogators who sometimes find one or two contradictions in a suspect's story and, during further interrogation, keep returning to those contradictions and so widen the gap of contradiction. This makes the gap more and more obvious, which becomes ever more painful to the suspect, who eventually may break down and confess. Such a confession is of limited value, as it may arise from inability to tolerate the pain of uncertainty arising out of the contradiction. That is one reason why, in a civilized country, limits are put on the amount of pressure that may be applied during interrogation. Even so, such an example impresses on the mind how deep is the need for unity. Truly, it is the deepest need of all because at bottom we *are* one.

This becomes apparent if we turn our attention to religion. God is One. "Hear! Oh hear, Oh Israel, the Lord thy God, the Lord is One," is the way the Jewish religion would put it. One could say that religion arises out of this deep need we all have for unity. In times of stress and confusion many people turn to religion in the hope that by doing so harmony will be restored. We gave some reasons for this when we said earlier that a person who cannot settle on one thing or another becomes anxious. The feeling of uncertainty is a most painful one. For example, many families in the United States still have a loved one missing in action from the Vietnam War. Most of them would say, "If only I knew, one way or the other!" Anxiety, or dukkha, as we know, is the basis of life, and the turn to Unity as God is a natural result. However, the anxiety that drives us to religion, to that which is of ultimate concern, is far deeper than anxiety coming from experience. It comes from the *nature* of experience itself.

But what if unity is divided against itself, not conceptually in the world of thought and ideas, but existentially; not as a unity split in half, but as *two unities*? Put differently, what if the split does not come as an experience of division, but as a division in the very way we experience? It would be like two different people sharing the same individuality. They would have entirely different experiences, yet would be the same person. We are not talking about a person being able to experience himself or herself as subject and object. That is already far downstream of this basic division.

That it is possible for two persons to share one individuality is confirmed by the reports, increasing in number, of people having multiple personalities. There are many accounts of people having a Dr. Jekyl-Mr. Hyde personality. Some have dozens of person-alities! If one reads the accounts carefully, however, one realizes that it is not a question of multiple *personalities* but of multiple *persons*. Many psychiatrists and psychologists, unable to accept the reports of multiple personalities, put the phenomenon down to the imagination of the patient and the gullibility of other ther-apists. The whole idea, when one grasps it, is so shocking because it violates our very idea, that we hold onto so dearly, of what is meant by being "an individual." However, in this, as in so many other instances, the pathological simply exaggerates the normal and does not replace it.

Three in One

We said that unity underlies all that we see, think, and understand. Now we are saying this One is two. Later we shall see further that this One is not one but *three*. If you are a Christian you will already have had some exposure to this possibility, but as a dogma. This dogma is the Trinity: God the Father, God the Son, and God the Holy Spirit. As a mystery, the Trinity cannot be expressed in consciousness, yet while this is true, a Trinity of another similar kind is the very basis of our conscious life itself.

Some Exercises

To think about what is being said is not enough. As we will show, this thinking, really our whole conscious life, has in part been established to protect us from the very implications of what we are talking about. On/off thinking, which we normally use to solve problems, would deny the very essence of what is being said, and not a few readers might well heave a sigh of exasperation when reading that one is not one but two! All I can do is to ask for the readers' goodwill and patience.

In the last chapter we promised to give some simple exercises to help overcome the limitations of logical, on/off thinking. Please take the time to do them as they are presented; although they are very simple they will help you encounter the problem in a way that is simply not possible conceptually. You may want to spend a few moments counting or following your breath to settle your mind.

Let us return to what we said at the beginning of the chapter: *we always see one*; one desk, one chair, one room. Please pick out an object, that is, be aware of it. (As we go through the exercise be sure you verify for yourself each step of the way.) If I may make a suggestion, you could choose this book you are reading; however, it does not have to be this; you may choose any object. The object, the book, is one is it not? It has boundaries that define it.

Now be aware of the room you are sitting in. Be aware of it as a whole. It too is one, one room. Now return your awareness to the object, and go back and forth between it and the room until you have the feel of what it means to say the object is one and the room as a whole is one.

Having done that, let me ask you what happens to your awareness as it goes from the book to the room and back? Maybe you would like to repeat the exercise to check what happens. Is it not that when you are aware of the object the awareness is *focused*, but when you are aware of the room the awareness

62

is *expanded*? Furthermore, a certain mental effort is necessary to focus, whereas to expand awareness this effort is relaxed; but, and please verify this, *this relaxation is also its own type of effort.* If one returns to the object, this effort in turn must be relaxed.

All this is quite elementary; there is nothing unusual in it. It is something you know full well and is simply being brought to your attention. But even so, please do this little exercise once or twice more so you get used to it.

Now please focus your attention even more and *pick out a part* of the object. If you have chosen the book then you could focus your attention on a word; if the object is a chair, you can focus on a leg. This, as you will see, calls for a little more effort. Now please expand your awareness and, instead of simply seeing the room as one, see the house or building the room is in as one. Again this calls for more effort of relaxation. Now focus your mind even further to, say, a letter of the word you have chosen, and now even further yet to a period ending the sentence. Now expand your attention to include the area or street the house is in and then to include the city, then the country, then the whole world. On each occasion there is a characteristic effort that is progressively increased to focus more or to expand awareness more, as the case may be. There is also a characteristic relaxation when changing from focus to expansion and back.

The Discovery and Creation of Unity

As maybe you have begun to see, the object, the book or the chair, is not one simply because it *is* one, but also because *you make it* one. Have you noticed (and if not, will you verify) that when you look at the room, the object, whatever it was you chose, sinks into and merges with the background and simply becomes another indistinguishable part of the whole that is called "a room"? Furthermore, until you focus your attention on it, the period ending the sentence is merged with the whole.

You can verify this by picking out still a different object. Now this object stands out, whereas it had just been an indistinguishable part of the whole. In other words, after you have put your attention on an object *it exists*. The original meaning of the word "exist"[2] is "to stand out." However, the point we are making is that not only does it exist, but it exists as *one*.

If you *name* the object it stands out even more readily, and furthermore, it cannot slip back quite so far into the background. If you would like to verify this, pick out a piece of the pattern in the carpet, or a stain on the wall or ceiling, or something similar that is usually overlooked, then give it a name, call it Bill or Susanne. Then, every now and again, refer to it by name. You will find it will take on an independent existence. *To name it is to give it an identity, to make it a permanent one.*

So the first thing our exercise shows is oneness is both discovered and created. Oneness is inherent in all things and so can be discovered. However, it is by picking it out from its surroundings that *you* create the book, the chair, the leg, the world, the room, the city, or whatever it is, and give it the special status of being one. It has its own unity intrinsically, but it awaits an awareness, in this case, your awareness, before this unity can be realized, before it becomes real. Making it real is an act of creation. There is a magic in this that we have become so used to that we do not appreciate it anymore.

Let us not forget, although we say the world is both created and discovered, there is all the difference between creation and discovery. A world that is discovered is there independent of you, but the world that you create is entirely dependent on you.

---

2   *Ex,* "out," *sistere,* "to stand."

The Two Viewpoints of Unity

We can see something more from this simple exercise. When you go from being aware of the object, say the book, to being aware of another object, say the chair, what is involved is a shift of focus. But when you go from being aware of the *object* to being aware of the *room*, it is no longer simply a change in focus that occurs; it is also *a change in location of the viewpoint,* but *without that location moving in any way.* Please go through the exercise once more and see what I mean. When you see the object, the viewpoint is *outside* what you are seeing. When you see the room the viewpoint is *inside.*

Are you the body? With this question you will see more clearly what I mean about these two viewpoints. You can say, "Yes, I am the body." In this case you are, so to say, inside the body. Or you can say, "No, I am not the body," in which case you are, so to say, outside the body looking at it as an object. One can say quite legitimately, "I am tired," which is an expression of the first point of view, or "My body is tired," which is an expression of the second, but much more is involved than simply a change of words.

Again this is very elementary and obvious, so much so you probably never give it any attention. But, and this is important to note, the two viewpoints *are incompatible with each other.* So much is this the case that when the inside viewpoint is adopted, the outside viewpoint *does not exist,* and vice versa. We are familiar with this type of thing from our discussions about the ambiguity of the vase and two faces. However, now we are talking about an *ambiguity that is at the very basis of our consciousness.* Furthermore, because it is at the very basis of awareness, everything we know and experience is affected by it. They are two equally valid viewpoints, but they are incompatible. If you reflect on this you will realize it is as though some geological fault runs through our entire conscious life. It is as though we are wounded in our very depths.

As the full implication of this is so crucial to all that is to come, to the whole understanding of ourselves and others, of our separation and of our suffering, let me quote from the work of a famous psychiatrist, R. D. Laing, for support (emphasis mine):

> A human being can be seen from two different points of view and one or other aspect can be made the focus of study. In particular, the human being can be seen as a person or as a thing. Now, even the same thing, seen from *two entirely different points of view*, gives rise to *two entirely different descriptions*, and the descriptions give rise to *two entirely different theories*, and the theories result in *two entirely different sets of action*. There is no dualism in the sense of the coexistence of two different essences or substances there in the object, psyche and soma; there are *two different experiential Gestalt: person and organism.*[3]

Another simpler way of putting this last sentence is there is not a mind and a body, a soul and a body, there is no ghost in the machine, to refer to the expression used in the introduction, but two different ways of looking at the same phenomenon. This means the question, "Is the body real and the mind an outcome of the body, or is the mind real and the body the outcome of the mind?" is meaningless and so can never be answered. *There is no body as a constant external object, nor is there a mind as a constant internal subject;* instead there are two mutually dependent but mutually exclusive viewpoints.

Most people when thinking or talking about the mind and the body think they are two independent things, two entirely different realities, the reality of the soul or mind and the reality of the body. It is said, for example, that the soul leaves the body at death. Also there are many arguments about whether the body gives birth to the mind or the mind gives birth to the body.

---

3   R. D. Laing, *The Divided Self* (Harmondsworth: Pelican Books, 1965), p. 20.

Theories that hold for the former are often called materialist, those that support the latter, idealist. But these statements about a body and a mind are meaningless. To ask these questions is like asking whether the vase is the real picture and the two faces dependent on it, or vice versa.

A Zen koan has this very enigma as its theme. It says, "Sei and her soul are separated; which is the real Sei?" The question which is the real Sei is asked knowing that neither the one nor the other is the true Sei. Yet even so, which is the true Sei?

Incidentally, a Zen master commenting on this koan said,

> Ever the same the moon among the clouds;
> Different from each other the valley and the mountain.
> How wonderful! How blessed!
> Is this one is this two?

Two Ones

Although what we have said so far is important, we have not yet exhausted the insights our exercise has to offer. During the exercise we saw the book as one, then the word as one, then the letter as one, then the period as one. This came from focusing awareness more and more. As we said earlier, this oneness is not simply a property of the object. Therefore there is nothing to stop awareness reducing its focus until it focuses on *a point without dimension*. This dimensionless point is One. In a similar way, when the mind is expanded, there is nothing to stop the awareness expanding its focus until it includes all that is without limit. Again this unlimited whole is One. Therefore we have two situations: a dimensionless point viewed from outside and an unlimited whole viewed from inside. Both are the One: Which now is the true One? These two Ones are obviously not the same; they are quite different. How is this possible? While you see the word "One" as simply a label, there is no problem. But if you have done the exercises attentively, you would have seen that while One *cannot be* both, yet One *is* both. It must be stressed that this is not a problem that I am just now inventing; it has a very long history. For example, a writer points out "this paradox [of the two Ones] is already contained within the Pythagorean cosmogony in the idea that the One, as monad, sometimes represents the one original *arche* of the world and sometimes reveals itself as the generating seed (thus revealing only one side of its two antithetical series)."[4] The word paradox should be understood in its original meaning as *beyond ideas, beyond thought and consciousness.*

The very basis of our awareness is everything is one. This we said is the basis of thinking itself. Yet this unity is undermined not only by awareness which, as we have seen, having two viewpoints is two, but even by Oneness itself, which also is two.

The Third One

Do you remember we said One is not one but three? We have now found two of these three ones. They are both one but different from each other. The first arises from a focusing awareness, which we could call active, or, for the moment, Yang. The second is an inclusive awareness that is all-embracing, which we could call passive, and so Yin. They are mutually exclusive but mutually dependent, as are Yin and Yang, and the faces and the vase.

We must now talk about the third One, and please be ready for a shock. Using the Yin-Yang terminology, we said Yin is the One; it is the whole. We also said Yang is the One; it too is the whole. But there is also Tao. Tao too is the whole. It too is the One. Yang is the exclusive One of the dimensionless point, Yin is the inclusive all-embracing One. What type of One is Tao? We cannot say that it is the One that includes Yin and Yang

---

4   Marie-Louise von Franz, *Number and Time* (Evanston, Ill.: Northwestern University Press, 1974), p. 62 n.

because Yin is the inclusive One. We cannot say it is the One that excludes, or is outside, Yin and Yang; Yang is the exclusive One.

Do you remember when we were discussing the symbol for Yin and Yang we said it would be a mistake to draw the outer circle to depict Tao? Tao is that out of which Yin and Yang emerge. *Tao is not separate from but not identical to Yin-Yang.* We cannot say it is neither Yin nor Yang and we cannot say it is both. If we were to draw a circle around the Yin-Yang symbol to indicate Tao it would imply that Tao is separate. How then are we to depict Tao?

The Dog and the Stone

A famous Hindu saying goes, "Dog no stone; stone no dog." Maybe it can help you see into what we are getting at. It seems to be talking about someone going home one night. A dog was barking at him but he could not find a stone to throw at it. Then later, when the dog had given up his barking, the person came across a stone.

However, the saying has another meaning. Suppose you are looking at a marble figure of a dog. You could admire the beauty of its form, the clean and intricate way the sculptor achieved the effects, the beauty of the dog. Or you could look at the marble and enjoy the smoothness of its surface and the beautiful veins that run through it. In the first case you see the dog but do not see the stone. In the second you see the stone but not the dog.

In this analogy Tao corresponds to the stone, to what one might call the substance, and Yin-Yang to the dog, to the form. Just as when one looks at the stone one does not notice the dog, so when one sees Tao one does not take Yin-Yang into account; when one takes into account Yin-Yang, the form, one does not see Tao.

Another more immediate analogy is the following: As you read this book you are aware of what it is about, but you take no notice of the paper on which it is printed. When you do take note of the paper the meaning of the book is lost.

What this implies, and this is why I warned you there was a shock in store, is we have yet *another* ambiguity. This time, however, it is an ambiguity within an ambiguity.

Yin and Yang are ambiguous. This is expressed Yin/Yang, the slash (/) meaning ambiguous. But there is also an ambiguity in Tao and Yin/Yang. Using the notation we suggested, this could be expressed Tao-(Yin/Yang).

This means that there is an ambiguity within an ambiguity. *There is an ambiguity, one face of which says there is no ambiguity. This face itself is not unambiguous.* This face says *there is no ambiguity because all is One;* but as we are now aware One is not unambiguous: there is the One of wholeness, the inclusive One and the One of identity, the exclusive One.

This total ambiguity is the ku that, as you remember, Yasutani roshi talked about in an earlier quotation. He said that ku is "not mere emptiness. It is that which is living, dynamic, devoid of mass, unfixed, beyond individuality or personalitythe matrix of all phenomena. Here we have the fundamental principle of Buddhism." The ambiguity we have just described is arrested ku or arrested *dynamism;* or one could say that dynamism is flowing ambiguity. It is like ice and water. Ice is frozen water, water is flowing ice. Consciousness arises when words arrest the flow. We can only consciously experience what is frozen.

There is, however, nothing that flows. This "nothing that flows" is the third One.

It is like the haiku we quoted earlier:

No one
walks this path
this autumn evening.

70

True Nature

This no one is true nature. You cannot point to it, or describe it in any way. If you are asked about it you can only say, "I don't know." It is Tao. It is One, but beyond any possible conception of one or any possible awareness of one. This One is the third One. It is not phenomena, but it cannot be separated from phenomena. It is this one that causes the oscillation back and forth between the old lady and the young lady, between the vase and the two faces. It is the tenth person, the one who is never counted.

When we first introduced the ambiguous pictures we drew your attention to the fact that when you looked at them there was a buildup of tension until you shifted your attention to the other picture. If you were looking at the vase there would be a buildup of tension until you looked at the two faces, on which there would be a temporary discharge of tension. As you continued to look at the two faces tension would again build up until you shifted your attention and so on.

We said that these phenomena, the buildup of tension and the shift of attention, underlay the difficulty of meditation. The mind is always moving, thoughts always arising. We can now say this movement of the mind happens because of the constant endeavor to embrace both Ones, the inclusive One and the exclusive One, simultaneously. By this endeavor we freeze the flow with words, ideas, thoughts, and images. But any success we have is illusory; change continues even while we call it change and so fix it in a concept. A philosopher named Zeno pointed this out a long time ago. He said that an arrow could never go from an archer to the target, because to do so it would have to pass through a halfway mark on the way to the target. But to pass this halfway mark it would have to pass through a halfway mark between the archer and the first halfway mark. But to do this _____. The arrow and everything else are therefore frozen into immobility. And yet the arrow finds its target.

Summary

We can now begin to glimpse how we separate ourselves from the ground of our being, and where original sin and the kleśa of ignorance come from. Separation arises out of two incompatible awarenesses. Because of their incompatibility they cannot both be present simultaneously, yet neither is secondary or inferior to the other. Each is Tao. Both have to be present; neither can give way to the other. Consciousness is the creation by which we try to overcome this impasse.

Chapter 6
The Center

Yet one more insight is to be gained from the exercise we have been doing. This one is so important we give it a chapter of its own. Although we will be repeating the main conclusions we came to during the last chapter, nevertheless there will be an addition. This addition will allow us, in the next chapter, to go full circle back to the story of Adam and Eve and to the kleśa of ignorance.

But first let me ask you yet another question. What do you think life would be like if it had no center?

To start with, we would have nowhere to go *to* and nowhere to go *from*. Nothing would be more important than anything else, and so nothing would have either meaning or value. There would be no beauty or truth, nothing good or holy. There would also be no past or future because there would be no present, and since there would be no future there would be nothing to look forward to. There would be no consciousness because there would be no integrating principle. In short, there would be nothing. The world would be dreamlike, confused, with a random and apparently accidental coming into being and passing away. You may be having some doubts about this, but what follows will explain it.

The Cosmic Center

Have you ever wondered why we have Christmas trees? Or why we put an angel on top of the tree, very often accompanied by a star? Why there are lights and tinsel, why the presents? Why is it that people used to dance, and still do dance, around the maypole on Mayday? Why did Native Americans dance around the totem pole? Why is it that periodically during the day devout Mohammedans will prostrate themselves toward Mecca and periodically undertake a pilgrimage there, ending the pilgrimage by circumambulating the Kaaba, a black rock considered by them to be sacred? Why is circumambulation considered to be a mark of respect and a way of greeting in some Eastern countries?

Do you see anything in common among these activities and events, or what they have to do with a center.

The Christmas tree is an embellished cosmic tree. The mythologist Mircea Eliade says that Vedic Indian, ancient Chinese, and German mythology, as well as the primitive religions, all had different versions of this cosmic tree, but in all versions the sacred tree was said to be at the *center of the world*. The maypole too represented the cosmic center as did the totem pole, which was another embellished cosmic tree. The dance around the tree was a ritual by which the participants drew power from the cosmic center while reaffirming it as the center. Moslems believe the Kaaba is the highest place on earth and faces the center of heaven. By facing it and bowing toward it, the devout reaffirm it as the center. Circumambulation also, whether by dancing or by walking, reaffirms the center.

By and large, our society has lost contact with ritual; it has become secular. Furthermore, the tendency is for scholars to rationalize the rituals of other societies and so reduce them to some other, more common, experience. For example, psychoanalysts would possibly say that the totem pole and the maypole were phallic symbols. Another way of psychologizing is to say these activities are related to archetypes. This is the Jungian approach. An archetype is a basic idea out of which, the Jungian says, our conscious life has evolved. Sometimes embedded in these ratio-nalizations is a tendency to look down on "primitive" people as being superstitious and ignorant, performing activities that we, with our superior wisdom, see as worthless. The reason we could let go of the tree as a sacred center is that we have introjected the center and now call it "I." The evolution of culture is the evolution of consciousness, and consciousness has evolved because of the steady introjection of the center as "I." For religious rituals we now have psychology and its many burgeoning offshoots in the New Age society, all paying homage to "I" as center and giving birth to the me generation.

The Reality of the Center

The center is real in its own right. The cosmic tree is not a symbol that *represents* the center. It *is* the center itself. Or maybe it would be better to say the tree is the incarnation of the center because, although it is the center, the center is not necessarily the tree. This might be more readily understood by an analogy.

Joe Brown may be the president of a company, but the president of that company is not *necessarily* Joe Brown, because Joe may be fired and Bill Smith appointed in his place. Just as several people in succession can be the president, so several things can be the center. The importance of this point is that although the center may appear in many guises, there is nevertheless only *one* center. However, the participants in the rituals do not *believe* that the tree is the center—they *know* it is so, just as the employees know (they do not believe) Joe Brown to be president.

The center is not an idea one believes in, but a certainty one has. It is not therefore a psychological reality, or an archetype any more than it is a physical thing or a property of physical things. It is the basis of consciousness, part of the structure that makes "I," the world, and God possible.

The center can be likened to the point of equilibrium of forces in a field. For example, children's playgrounds often have teeter-totters, or see-saws. The teeter-totter is centered on a point of equilibrium. This center is real since it exerts a direct influence, but look as you will you will not find its existing anywhere, neither in the wood of the teeter-totter nor anywhere else.

However, the center we are talking about is not simply a passive element like the center of the teeter-totter; it is an active source having its own energy. In our discussion of the center we will also discuss this energy. Because many different cultures have known of this energy, it has come to have several different names. It has been called, among other things, *baraka, mana, prana,* and *ki.* Many people know ki from the practice of *aikido,* a very popular form of the martial arts. In Zen this energy is called joriki. In our culture it has been given names such as the odic force, orgone energy, L fields, and so on.

You will not be surprised, or, I hope by now, dismayed, to learn that although, as I have said, there can only be *one* dynamic center, we shall identify *three.* We will show it is out of the struggle between two of these centers to be *the* dynamic center that a third is born, or, better still, is constantly in the process of being born.

The Importance of the Center

But before going on, let us talk generally about the center so you will have a better idea of it. As with much that we have discussed, the center is so ubiquitous, so totally taken for granted, that it is constantly overlooked, and thus difficult to talk about. In the following discussion, we will be drawing to some extent on the work of Mircea Eliade, a well-known Romanian mythologist, whom we have already quoted.

For the ancients, the establishment of a stable center was a matter of deep concern because "nothing can begin, nothing can be done without a previous orientation, and any orientation implies getting a fixed point. This is why religious man has always sought to fix his abode at the center of the world."[1] However, the establishment of a fixed point must have suprahuman sanction, and it can only be discovered through the help of secret signs: "When no sign manifests itself it is provoked. A sign is asked to put an end to the tension and anxiety caused by relativity and disorientation, in short to reveal an absolute point of support."[2]

For example, to provoke such a sign, a wild animal is hunted and a sanctuary is built at the place where it is killed. Or a domestic animal such as a bull is turned loose; some days later it is searched for and sacrificed at the place where it is found. Later an altar will be raised there and a village built around it. Human beings are not free to *choose* the center; they only search for it and find it by the help of mysterious signs.

These quotations help us to understand the importance of the center. Without it there is no world, everything falls into chaos, and life as we know it is impossible. However, as these quotations point out also, it is not *anything* that can be the center. The center gives the importance to things, therefore things cannot create a center. This is why the center has to *appear*, or, using Eliade's words, it has to have suprahuman sanction.

The Achilpa tribe has a sacred pole that represents the cosmic axis, or world center. This pole was fashioned by their ancestor from a gum tree. After anointing the pole with blood, the ancestor climbed it and disappeared into the sky. The pole was, in this way, uniquely designed by the ancestor as the center. It was he who gave it suprahuman sanction. During their wanderings the tribe always carried the pole with them and would choose the direction they were to take by the direction in which it bent.[3]

---

1   Mircea Eliade, *The Sacred and the Profane* (New York: Harvest Books, 1957), p. 22.

2   *Ibid.*, p. 27.

The world center is not a geographical center but a *dynamic* center, and, as we have said, *there can only be one such center*. If there were more than one a terrible conflict would arise over which was the real one. This is quite evident when we consider human societies and groups. It is axiomatic a group can have only one leader; for example, only one president of a company. A leader is the center, the source of initiative, and at the center of the lines of communication of the group. The role of the leader is most often implicit during times of no apparent conflict, but during times of stress and confusion this role becomes very active. Even in space vehicles, which might have only two crew members, one is always appointed the leader. Revolts happen when, in addition to an existing leader, another arises to challenge him or her. When this happens and until the dispute is settled, there will be confusion and even chaos in the group.

It is evident, then, the loss of the sacred pole would be a terrible tragedy to the Achilpa tribe, as it would open the members to an infinite number of potential candidates to be the center, each opposing the others. This would generate anxiety and panic. Indeed, Eliade said, "For the pole to be broken denotes catastrophe; it is like 'the end of the world,' reversion to chaos."[4] Once, according to some anthropologists who observed this tribe, when the pole was broken, the entire clan was in consternation; "They wandered about aimlessly for a time and finally lay down on the earth together and waited for death to overtake them."[5]

In case someone should think this is simply an aberration of a single primitive people, we must remember that throughout history, and in all kinds of societies, it has been the practice to

---

3   *Ibid.*, p. 33.

4   *Ibid.*

5   *Ibid.*

carry a banner into battle. This banner is but an ornate pole. If it were captured by the enemy, the army would collapse, and panic and chaos follow. To carry the banner into battle was both an honor and a great danger. It was an honor because it meant one's valor had been recognized; it would be a great danger because the one carrying the banner would be a prime target. Even in our sophisticated and cynical culture the flag is still sacred to many people for whom it is the center of power of the group.

Furthermore, people who have become lost in a forest have panicked and died of fear. They were lost because all trees looked alike to them and none had special value. Therefore none could represent the center.

The Incarnation of the Center

The Christmas tree is a relic of the cosmic tree. The star on the tree is also a relic of the cosmic center: the north star. Travelers for eons would guide themselves by reference to it. A person lost in the woods has only to wait until the stars come out to find his orientation. With the aid of the star one knows where one *is*. Later, magnetic north, indicated by a compass, replaced the stars and travelers were able to steer their way even in cloudy and foggy conditions. Because the compass always points to the north pole, that is, always points to a magnetic center, travelers always know where they are.

The angel on the Christmas tree is a relic of a time when the tree was the center and so had a numinous quality. It had this numinous quality because it was not merely alive but was the source of life itself. This does not mean the tree is the source of life, but the source of life is manifest through the tree, or, as we said earlier, is incarnate in the tree. Later this numinous quality was enhanced by having images of sacred, that is totem, animals and figures carved into the tree, or by replacing the tree with a sacred statue that then became an idol. The word "idol" comes from a Greek word that means *form*.

This appearance of the life source in form is called theophany. The religious person sees that the life source and its many forms are the *same* but, at the same time, that they are also quite *different*. The most celebrated theophany in the West is the appearance of Christ, who, the Christians say was God made man, or in the words we have been using, the life source made man. The mystery of the Incarnation has taxed theologians throughout the centuries. Was Christ God or was he man? St. John says in his gospel, "In the beginning was the word and the word was *with* God and the word *was* God." To be "with God" would mean to be different from God; but nevertheless, as it says in the gospel, the word *was* God. Therefore St. John was saying in effect *Christ was both God and different from God.* In the same way Joe Brown is the president and different from the president; the tree is the center and different from the center.

The reason for lights on the Christmas tree is that since time immemorial people have recognized the affinity between awareness and light. It might even be said awareness is the subjective experience of light or light is the objective experience of awareness. When Christ said, "I am the light of the world," he spoke for each one of us. Each of us is the light by which all lights get their brilliance. The references to light in sacred literature are so many it is impossible to know where to start, but as this subject was dealt with in *The Iron Cow of Zen*, we will not dwell on it now.

The gifts on the Christmas tree, particularly the fruits and sweets, come from the realization we are sustained at every level by the center: that the gift of life is a gift of the center. But this is putting into words what cannot really be given form.

So the tree, the angel, the star, the lights, the gifts all attest to the fact the tree is special. It is (or, I should say, was) the cosmic center and so the source of life, consciousness, and society. Few people do not, at some level of their being, respond to the magic of the Christmas tree.

Going Up Is Going to the Center

Not only trees and human beings but mountains and buildings also were, and sometimes still are, looked on as being at the center of the world. To quote again from Eliade, "In a number of cultures we hear of such mountains, real or mythical, situated at the center of the world."[6] Islamic tradition says that the highest place on earth is the Kaaba, because "The pole star bears witness that it faces the center of heaven."[7] For the Christian, Golgotha is on the summit of the cosmic mountain.

That a mountain is a cosmic center means that by going up, we go *nearer the center*, and by going down we go *away from* the center. To go up is to go to heaven, to go down is to go to hell. This relationship between level and the center and the importance of the center enables us to understand so much about human behavior. For example, and just one among a multitude, it helps us understand why some people bow to others. By bowing we raise reciprocally the one to whom we bow, and by raising we place the one who was raised at the center. If you saw Polanski's film *Macbeth* you may remember MacDuff was proclaimed king not by his subjects bowing, but by his standing at the center of a round shield and being raised to shoulder height by his followers.

The Temple as Center

Temples are replicas of the cosmic mountain. This too will help one understand the behavior of people. It explains why builders gave so much attention to the choice of the proper site for a temple or church, why they labored so hard in its construction,

---

6   *Ibid.*, p. 38.

7   *Ibid.*

and even why so much emphasis was placed on getting the steeple to be so high.

"The first sign a temple is under construction is the 'pillar' is erected at the sacred center. . . . It is around this center the church is built."[8] These quotations come from Louis Charpentier, who was writing about the construction of Chartres Cathedral. He also points out in the same book that there was a group of Notre Dame churches in France oriented with reference to the constellation Virgo, or the Virgin, and they form the pattern of this constellation on earth. The Tor in Somerset, England, the highest mound created by humans, is at the center of a huge zodiac carved in the surrounding countryside, and Stonehenge was built so that at the equinoxes the sun and all the heavens confirm the site as being at the center of the world.

The Center in Modern Times

In case we smile indulgently at the ancients, let us give some instances of the power of the center in modern times. As we said, a person can become the world center. This may help explain why so often a company president's office is on the top floor, and why the office next to it is coveted by other executives. Those who remember the early negotiations between the Americans and the North Vietnamese for peace will remember there was much discussion about the table, and eventually the delegates chose a round table. The one who sits at the head of the table is the center, and those who sit next to the center are more important than others sitting farther away. It also explains why it is important who goes to whose office. The center, by definition, cannot move because whatever moves does so in reference to

---

8   Louis Charpentier, trans., *The Mysteries of Chartres Cathedral* (London: Sir Ronald Fraser Throston's Publishing, 1966), p. 84.

the center. Whoever goes to the other therefore acknowledges the other as center.

The center, because it is the source of life, has healing power, and the power of healing of some saints came from their being the center. Kings too, whose crown, scepter, and orb proclaimed them world center, in former times were expected to lay their hands on the heads of their subjects who were sick, and so heal them. Lourdes and other pilgrimage sites are centers and it is from this they get their power to heal. Pilgrims who have to overcome great hardship to reach a holy site constantly reaffirm the power of the center. This center in turn enables them to overcome the suffering they undergo to reach the site.

When saints died it was the practice to keep their relics as sacred centers. These would be enshrined in churches and so enhance the importance of churches as pilgrimage sites. The importance of relics became such in the Middle Ages that a whole industry was devoted to their manufacture. In Montreal, St. Joseph's Oratory has the tomb of Brother André, a Catholic friar who was beatified because of his spiritual life and considerable power of healing. The Oratory is a pilgrimage site.

Nowadays it is not the saints who have the power of the center but politicians. Hitler was such a center for millions of Germans, and one example of his genius as a demagogue was that he intuitively realized the power of the center and used it in many different ways. For example, he would deliberately come late to a rally of thousands of followers. The place he was to fill would stand vacant, and because of the vacancy the place would acquire an aura of its own. He would then arrive by airplane and, so to say, descend to earth from on high to take up this place, which would then become not simply the focal center, but also the dynamic center of this enormous crowd, each person in which would affirm the power of the center.

Not only politicians but also film stars and rock singers are taking over the power of the center. The cults of Marilyn Monroe and Elvis Presley are two well-known examples. The hysteria of the crowd in the presence of such idols is the same as that found at some religious festivals. Relics are now buttons ripped off coats and watches snatched from wrists. Can you imagine the prestige someone would gain if he or she could say, "This was Elvis Presley's watch," or "This was Marilyn's comb."

A striking example of this phenomenon was Charles Lindbergh's arrival in Europe after flying solo across the Atlantic in 1927. About 200,000 people were there to welcome him in Paris; in London there were well over 100,000. One correspondent described the scene in Paris as Lindbergh landed:

> There is pandemonium, wild animals let loose and stampede towards the plane . . . running people ahead running people all around and the crowd behind stampeding like buffalo . . . the extraordinary impression I had of hands thousands of hands weaving like maggots over the silver wings [of the plane] and it seems to me as if all the hands in the world are touching or trying to touch the new Christ and the new Cross is the Plane and knives slash at the fuselage hands multiply every where scratching tearing. . . .[9]

The slashing knives were cutting off relics, now known as souvenirs. The author of the book from which this excerpt was taken said:

> Lindbergh had become Everyman, and Everyman had become Lindbergh. He was literally worshipped and adored. People sought relics from his person and his plane as if he were some new god.[10]

---

9   Modris Ecksteins, *The Rites of Spring: The Great War and the Birth of the Modern Age* (Lester and Orpen Dennys, 1990), p. 243.

10   *Ibid.*, p. 244.

The Paradox of the Center

We have said enough to show that the center has enormous integrating power. As Eliade said, "There is something in the human condition that we may call *the nostalgia for Paradise*. By this we mean the desire to find oneself always and without effort at the center of the world, at the heart of Reality."[11]

However, there is a strange paradox here: Everyone is already *at* the center of the world and yet each person is constantly *striving to reach it*. Eliade says:

> We observe one group of traditions attests the desire of man
> to find himself without effort at the center of the world,
> whilst another group insists upon the difficulty and conse-
> quently the merit of being able to enter into it.[12]

Do we not have a contradiction here? A whole array of myths, symbols, and rituals emphasize with one accord *the difficulty of entering into a center*; while on the other hand another series of myths and rites lays it down that *this center is immediately accessible*:

> The way which leads to the center is sown with obstacles
> and yet every city, every temple, every dwelling is already
> at the center of the universe. The sufferings and the trial of
> Ulysses are fabulous; nevertheless any return to hearth and
> home whatever is equivalent to Ulysses' return to Ithaca.[13]

Some Examples

To help you truly grasp this essential paradox and to bring it all down to earth, let me ask you to suppose (or visualize)

---

11   Mircea Eliade, *Images and Symbols*, trans. Philip Mairet (London: Harvill Press), p. 55.

12   *Ibid.*

13   *Ibid.*, p. 54.

you are out for a walk in the country on a fine spring morning. It is warm, the sun is shining, a slight breeze is blowing. The birds sing out and the flowers nod their heads yellow, blue, mauve, and red. The peace of the moment overtakes you. Then someone suddenly calls out, "Hey!" Maybe you could visualize this type of situation a couple of times and observe what happens to your awareness, and what happens to your feelings when you change from being sunk into the moment to being alert to that sudden call.

Do you find a difference in the quality of your awareness? Do you feel any pain at the changeover? Perhaps try again. At first you are, as it were, at the center of a globe of awareness. In the second the "Hey!" is at the center and you are on the outside looking in. That is what is meant by a change in the quality of awareness.

Another example: Have you ever been walking in the prairie, or maybe on an ocean liner that is way out at sea? If you have you will know the feeling of being at the center of a huge plate. Then if, for example, an airplane flies over, or if you are in the prairie and pass by a farmhouse, that can become the center and you are now on the outside looking in.

Let us now try something more immediate. As you sit there now, feel yourself to be the center of the world. All the sights are coming to you, all the sounds, all the smells, even the sensations of your body. The past stretches back from where you are and the future stretches ahead. Feel yourself as the center of the world.

Now pick something in the room, a chair, an ornament, a hi-fi knob, and see that as the center of the world. Do this several times and feel the change of viewpoint.

Then try the following: Feel you are the body or you are in the body looking out. Now feel you are not the body, that the body is an object among other objects you can observe.

These exercises show there are two equally valid centers. The first is the center that one *is*; the second is the center of which one is at the periphery. This will enable us to understand what Eliade means when he speaks of the contradiction:

> We observe one group of traditions attests the desire of man to find himself without effort at the center of the world, whilst another group insists upon the difficulty and consequently the merit of being able to enter into it.[14]

The Difficulty of Demonstration

What we want to do is to show there are *two* centers when we have said there can only possibly be one. As we will see, this is a refinement of the problem that we discussed in the last chapter, the problem of the two Ones, and will involve equally paradoxical conclusions. This demonstration also will not be easy.

Let us repeat, because it is basic, that the conflict between the two Ones and therefore between these two centers is at the source of all our suffering, including the most agonizing and the most horrifying. All the hatred, anger, fear, and anguish the world has ever known has its origin here. One of the ways this conflict is resolved, as we have already said, is through consciousness, consciousness that is a continuous creation. However, I can only address you, the reader, through consciousness—your consciousness and mine. That is why the demonstration will be difficult. All the words I use already shroud, and are specifically designed to shroud, this conflict, this fundamental wound, this "Adam's curse." It takes courage to suspend, even for a moment, the creation called consciousness, to bring the mind to a halt, and glimpse what lies beyond.

The Buffer of Consciousness

A woman wrote the following about consciousness protecting us from Adam's curse by the center or "I":

14　*Ibid.*, p. 55.

Suddenly I was aware that all life around me had come to a complete standstill. Everywhere I looked, instead of life, I saw a hideous nothingness invading and strangling the life out of every object and vista in sight. It was a world being choked to death by an insidious void, whereby every remaining movement was but the final throes of death. The sudden withdrawal of life left in its wake a scene of death, dying and decay so monstrous and terrible to look upon I thought to myself: no man can see this and live! My body froze to the spot.

The immediate reaction was to ward off the view, to make the vision go away by finding some explanation or meaning for it; in a word, to rationalize it away. Just as I reached for each defense, the knowledge that I had not a single weapon dawned in me like a sudden blow to the head, and in the same instant I understood this thing called self; it is man's defense against seeing absolute nothingness, against seeing a world devoid of life, a world devoid of God. Without a self, a man is defenseless against such a vision, a vision he cannot possibly live with.[15]

We can understand this condition if we realize that, for one reason or another, the center was no longer present. As she says, "Without a self [a center] a man is defenseless against such a vision."

What must also be stressed is that she says, "The immediate reaction was to ward off the view, to make the vision go away by finding some explanation for it; in a word to rationalize it away." Words are our great ally and they are essential ingredients in the creation called consciousness. Through consciousness words give us experience and existence. We got an inkling of this in the last chapter when we were exploring oneness and named a

---

15   Bernadette Roberts, *The Experience of No-Self* (Boulder, Colo.: Shambhala, 1984), p. 43.

part of the carpet or a stain. Buddhism teaches that consciousness arises out of *nama* and *rupa* ("name" and "form"), and they arose out of consciousness. Nonetheless, *words separate us from ourselves,* from our true home. They cast us out of the garden of Eden and entrench our ignorance.

All this goes to show why, as I said, it will be difficult to demonstrate the truth of this statement so full of contradiction: *There are two centers, but it is only possible to have one.*

Why Only One Center?

But let us ask why can there be only one center?

When Buddha was born he took seven steps and, pointing with one hand to the heavens and with the other to the earth, exclaimed, "Throughout heaven and earth I alone am the honored One." A great Zen master, Ummon, said, "If I had been there I should have knocked him dead with a single blow. This would have been some contribution to the harmony of the world."

"I alone am the honored One." Peerless without compare, unlimited, vaster than vast. Each of us is the honored *One.* But to say it is to defile it. To speak the truth is to defile the truth. That is what Ummon means. If I say, "You are not a man or a woman, you are not a person, a Canadian or an American, a Russian or a Frenchman, you are not a human being," there is something that responds, but, also, there is bewilderment. "If I am not a human being, what am I?" "What am I?" The response to this question is so intimate and so obvious even the question is too much. So much so is this the case that as I write and you read we wander farther and farther away from the truth. Do you remember the monk who went to the master and was just going to ask a question when the master hit him? What a wonderful response. Even to open the mouth is too much.

This is not a philosophical abstraction. Please do not think it is something too difficult. On the contrary, the problem is that it is too simple. It is so simple that we make desperate efforts to grasp "it." It is this grasping that gives birth to the third center incarnate in the cosmic tree, the cosmic mountain, the world center, and so on. The center is the emissary of the honored One, in the same way Christ is the incarnation of God. As the emissary of Oneness it can only be One—single, undivided, and indivisible.

This center is like a mustard seed, infinitesimal, but the source of all worlds. Meister Eckhart, the German mystic, quoting a Greek philosopher says:

> I am aware of something in me which sparkles in my intelligence; I clearly perceive that it is some what but what I cannot grasp. Yet methinks if only I could seize it I should know all truth.[16]

This seed, this sparkle, is One. It restores lost unity. Most of the religious practices of the human race maintain and restore the power of the center through ritual, ceremony, prayer, and fasting. Because of this power, the antagonism inherent in the two centers, one of which is me-as-center, the other, the unknown but ubiquitous me-as-periphery, is laid to rest.

Me-as-Center/Me-as-Periphery

As you have seen through the exercises suggested above, you are the center of the world. One appreciates this better by examining what one means when one says "me." "Me" is a witness of all, the basic point from which all is viewed. Me-as-center is the primary center of the world. It is the origin of all. There is not me here and the world over there. There is one undivided whole. This is why we use the clumsy expression me-as-center/me-as-periphery. To break up this whole is to kill it.

But, simultaneously, me is also at the periphery: I am sitting in the office. The phone rings. The boss says come. I go to the boss. The boss is the center. That is why we have leaders, to

---

16 Franz Pfeiffer, *Meister Eckhart* (London: John M. Watkins, 1956), p. 8.

provide a focal point, a center for a group. If one refuses to accept that, refuses to acknowledge the boss as center, then one no longer belongs to the group. With beehives this is brought home dramatically because should the queen bee, the boss, die, the hive dies also. The boss is outside, he or she is over there, and I am peripheral. To that extent the boss is center and I am periphery.

The problem with this example, and with all the examples that we are offering of me-as-center/me-as-periphery, is that the tension coming from the antagonism between the two has already been resolved in consciousness. The boss, insofar as he or she is *my* boss, is also me-as-center as well as me-as-periphery. This accounts for the tendency that many people have to idealize the boss in some way.

Another example, suffering from the same limitations but nevertheless useful, is that of a young child playing near its mother. If you are observant you will note that the child will run off and then run back to the mother, often allowing the distance both in time and space gradually to increase. Even when eventually settling down to play the child will throw glances repeatedly in the direction of the mother. Other examples are if we are going to catch a plane, the plane is the center. If we are going to the office, the classroom, or the studio, the office, the classroom, or the studio is the center to which "me" is peripheral.

What this means is that me-as-center is basic. But so is me-as-periphery. Neither one is derived from one or the other. However, *there is only one me*. Me is indivisible and so there can only be one center: *me-as-center* or *me-as-periphery*. Perhaps a diagram will help to make the point:

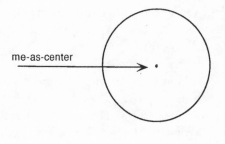

me-as-center

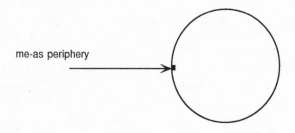

me-as periphery

Here we see two distinct me's, which as we said is not possible. Therefore we have to adopt a better way of illustrating the situation, which is the following:

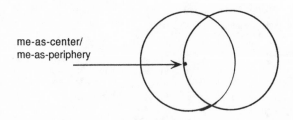

me-as-center/
me-as-periphery

The Participant and the Observer

Although we continue to use the expression me-as-center/me-as-periphery, it is so cumbersome that we will try to avoid it as much as possible. So let us try to find other words, but please keep in mind the expression and, as far as possible, what it means. When you imagined just now you were walking in the country it was as though you were a participant in, or part of, nature. The surroundings radiated from "me," their living center. This was me-as-center, and we can call this participant awareness or simply the *participant*. But when someone shouted, "Hey!" you were observer. This was me-as-periphery, and we could call it observer awareness or simply the *observer*.

Now, as we know, although these are by no means the same, we cannot separate them any more than we can separate the vase from the two faces. They are mutually exclusive but also mutually dependent. Our language forces us to talk as though we can make the separation, and it is in just this way it creates its protective barrier. But we must not lose sight of the truth that me-as-center/me-as-periphery are inextricably bound together, like oxygen and hydrogen are bound together as water. Nor can we say one of the modes, participant or observer, is the real one and the other false. Each has equal claim. *Each is a complete and whole way of seeing the world.* The scientific mode is primarily the mode of the observer. The scientist looks, as it were, at the world from outside. This is what is meant by being objective. However, when the scientist starts wondering whether he will receive a Nobel prize for the work he is doing, he slips into the participant mode.

Generally speaking, when we look at television or a film we are mainly in the participant mode. We enter the situation and become identified with it. We like to have the lights dimmed so we can do this more fully. If someone nearby scrunches popcorn or rustles paper it makes us irritable because it breaks the spell of participation.

This problem of ambiguity haunted an artist, Escher who was forever trying to find some way to transcend the dilemma and so unite it into a unity. One of his lithographs, *The Print Gallery*, has a direct bearing on what we are saying. One can see a man, an *observer*, who is looking at the picture but who is also a *participant* in the picture. What is most interesting in this picture is a "fudge" factor, a white circle in the middle of it. This fudge factor covers up the point of hiatus, the point of the jump. It disguises the impossibility of depicting a hiatus in the lithograph, an impossibility that arises out of the impossibility of being both the center and periphery simultaneously.

For a time it is as though one mode of awareness predominates over the other. For example, in a hockey game the players are mainly in the participant mode of awareness, the spectators in the observer mode. Notice that we say one mode of awareness *predominates* over the other, not that one replaces the other. Both modes are present, but not in the same way or with the same intensity or frequency.

Alternation Between Two Centers and the Creation of Consciousness

When you were looking at the ambiguous picture you experienced an alternation between the vase and the two faces. Without this alternation, unbearable tension would build up. Similarly, there is alternation between observer and participant that prevents the buildup of tension. It is the interruption of this tension that makes consciousness necessary; or, better still, consciousness-of-a-real-outer-world necessary.

Consciousness, as has been pointed out, etymologically means "I know together" (*con scio*), that is, "knowing together" or better still, "knowing as one whole." This knowing as one whole means that the center unites two disparate viewpoints into one whole: a-consciousness-of-the-real-outer-world. Again, the words are hyphenated to be sure that the mistake is not made of having a consciousness "here" and an outer world "there." Put slightly differently, there are no inner and outer worlds that are brought together in some magical fashion. For the dreamer, the visionary, and the hallucinator, the dream, the vision, and the hallucination are also all consciousness-of-the-real-outer-world.

The role of the center in the creation of consciousness will be discussed at length in a moment. But let us take note that consciousness is also being created constantly through the interaction of the observer and participant awareness. This interaction, in turn, gives the appearance of there being one viewpoint only, a viewpoint of *an ostensibly real outer world*.

An analogy involving binocular vision might help clarify this point. Close one eye and, with the other, look at two things, one behind the other. Then open that eye while closing the other, and repeat this for a few times. It appears one or the other or both of the things being looked at are moving. Binocular vision, which is how we see when both eyes are open, reconciles this instability in one stable view through the creation of *the third dimension*. Draftsmanship has uncovered for us the existence of the two centers that are resolved and generally absorbed in three-dimensional reality. These are called the two vanishing points, one of which is the point of perspective.

Similarly, consciousness reconciles participant and observer in the experience we know as reality. This reconciliation calls for a constant transition or leap from one side to the other from observer to participant, and this in turn requires effort. There is no gradient between being participant and being observer, any more than there is at any given moment between seeing the vase and seeing the two faces. The changeover is abrupt, on an all-or-nothing basis. *There is therefore, during the alternation, a moment when each has equal force.* This creates tension and the need for effort to transform the tension. It is just this tension and effort that give the characteristic tension and battle of life.

The struggle and battle are heightened because of an ever-present threat that neither of the two modes will give way to the other. Should this happen it is as though a revolt breaks out. This revolt has a variety of names—worry, anxiety, depression, and, in its severest form, a nervous breakdown.

This struggle of life takes on a further, bitter quality by the presence of others. As Sartre, the French philosopher, said, "Hell is other people." Understanding the connection between these two, the threat of civil war and Hell is other people, will make it possible to understand these concepts more clearly.

Hell Is Other People

The two centers can be reconciled through alternation, and alternation is possible because of time. Cycles of alternation pervade existence. Everything goes in cycles and a cycle is nature's way of reconciling two extremes through time. Time makes it possible to have night and day, summer and winter, and so on.

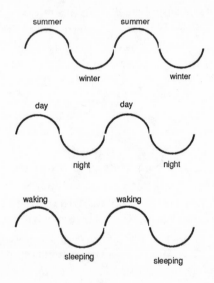

Now suppose time is not available; then, of course, alternation is not possible either. Let us see the implications of this.

A Conversation   Let us suppose you are to meet a friend for lunch. Naturally when you meet you will talk together. First you will say something, then your friend will say something in reply, then you will say something, and so on. That is the way a good conversation goes. After the lunch you will leave feeling good, quite relaxed. You will like your friend.

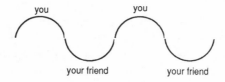

During the conversation, while you are talking, you are the center. This we have also called the participant; your friend is at the periphery, what we have called the observer (although here "listener" would be a better word). When your friend speaks it is reversed; your friend is at the center and you are at the periphery. Because of the alternation implicit in a conversation, the strain of holding the two modes together in consciousness is released a little. This is one important reason that we enjoy talking with one another. It is often unimportant what is said as long as each is willing and able to yield to the other. When this happens you and your friend are one whole.

The Confrontation of the Two Centers   Now suppose your neighbor's dog has been in your garden and has dug up your favorite flowers. You have to speak to your neighbor about this. How do you feel? Tense and uncomfortable. You do not like your neighbor as much as you did before the dog had its spree in the garden. When you speak to each other, instead of a conversation, it turns into an argument. You want to say something but the neighbor interrupts. And so you interrupt him. He raises his voice, saying, "You listen to me!" "No!" you say, "You listen to me!" And so it goes.

If you are observant you will notice you will avoid holding your neighbor's eyes for long. When your eyes and his do lock, be cautious, particularly if you both are men. Extreme anger and aggression build up, and will continue to build up as long as the eyes are locked. This tension could build to the point where one strikes out in anger and tries to destroy the other. Furthermore, the one who looks away first will feel as though he has lost in some way and will feel humiliated. The possibility of this cyclic buildup, and the resultant need to yield under pressure and look away, is why we avoid prolonged eye contact during an argument.

The argument most probably will end before any eruption. You might, for example, walk away from your neighbor in disgust. Then what happens next? You will seek out someone who is sympathetic to you and you will start destroying your neighbor's image. You will say something like, "Do you know, I think that guy next door is a bit crazy. He's certainly a big oaf. A bully, that's what he is. That's why he keeps that lousy dog. All I wanted to do. . . ."

And the neighbor? He too has found a sympathetic friend, and so it goes. Once upon a time one would have destroyed the neighbor in effigy as well as verbally. Witches used to get even with their enemies by making effigies and sticking pins in them. Even now, for example, during strikes, people vent their wrath on another by burning or hanging the person in effigy.

Why do we do this? Why do we verbally, in imagination, or in effigy, destroy our neighbor in this way? If one is attentive, one will see this type of mental aggression occupies much of our waking life.

We do it to try to overcome the buildup of unbearable tension brought about by the conflict of two centers, each vying to be the only one. Ostensibly these two centers are me and the neighbor. But in fact they are me-as-center/me-as-periphery, which are merely given form and expression by the neighbor and me the personality.

By trying to destroy the image of the neighbor, however, I reaffirm his presence, and a vicious circle results. It is like a spiritual hemorrhage. Hatred is an attempt to stop this hemorrhage. Hatred is like the bleeding of a wound that, when congealed, staunches itself. It comes out of the formula, "I hurt, it is your fault." Talking and thinking about our neighbor keeps up a steady flow of pain. However, we blame the neighbor, which is a forceful way of separating ourselves from him. In blaming, the pain turns to hate and so congeals. In hatred, because it is so dense and rigid, we find a secure center. However, hatred also causes separation, and so in itself becomes the cause of further pain. Once one sees this one can see the great wisdom in Christ's injunction, "Love thine enemy," because your enemy is the other half of yourself.

Let us continue with our inquiry and a quotation from R. D. Laing again:

> An argument occurred between two patients in the course of a session in an analytic group. Suddenly, one of the protagonists broke off the argument to say, "I can't go on. You are arguing in order to have the pleasure of triumphing over me. At best you win an argument. At worst you lose an argument. *I am arguing in order to preserve my existence.*"[17]

Why does considerable tension arise when we have to say disagreeable things to another person? How can we be engulfed by another? How can we lose our existence because of an argument? How can another's look create such pain that we are almost willing to destroy that person? It is the look that gives us the clue.

---

17 Laing, *The Divided Self*, p. 43.

Hostile eye contact with another arouses me-as-center/me-as-pe-riphery simultaneously. Alternation is no longer possible, and so the tension that has built up cannot be released. Put another way, the simultaneous arousal of me-as-center/me-as-periphery threatens to destroy the unity of "me." However, this unity cannot be destroyed. "Me " is the direct emissary of the One and cannot be divided. That fact, however, does nothing to reduce the *threat* of destruction, which therefore appears to increase reciprocally. This makes the threat more painful, which in turn increases the opposing force of unity. This in turn increases the threat, and so on. Here we have the spiritual counterpart to the old question that is, or used to be, asked in physics: What happens when an irresistible force meets an immovable object?

The Buffer of Consciousness

In the argument with the neighbor we have the possibility of turning away. We might say, "I've got better things to do than to argue with you." This turning away, or giving our attention to something else, is possible because of consciousness, with the concomitant ability to remember and imagine. With the help of language, thought, memory, and imagination, and with the help of the past and the future, we shield ourselves from the smoldering pain in the very heart of our being.

Consciousness has been acquired. As a human creation it has taken many, many hundreds of thousands of years to bring it laboriously into being. Each of us is heir to this work of ages. Each of us takes up this heritage through what is called "education." At the origin there is no consciousness. Our true nature is pure nonreflected awareness: in the words of Bodhidharma, *"vast emptiness and not a thing that can be called holy."* As a race our origin lies in the past; as an individual it is ever present. Presence is the source.

Pure nonreflected awareness also has the potential for awareness of awareness and, because of this, the potential for consciousness. But the potential for awareness of awareness is also the potential for engulfment. This, as we already pointed out, gives the ever-present sense of insecurity and vulnerability.

With a baby, there is a time before recourse to consciousness is possible. With a baby there is not yet the possibility of turning away and so breaking the deadlock. The irresistible force meets the immovable object. It is here the third center is born.

Let us then understand this birth of the third center and, as it is so important, we will take time to build up the background to make it easier to grasp.

The Birth of I-It

When we were discussing the dilemma, we pointed out that we are presented with alternatives, each of which has equal claim to be the only one possible. We gave as an example the dilemma of abortion. Let us suppose a woman is pregnant, but for one reason or another does not want to deliver the baby. In her eyes, it is a very good reason. Maybe her health is threatened. Let us suppose also this same woman has some equally good reasons for having the baby. Maybe she believes strongly in the sanctity of all life. She is faced by a terrible dilemma that can tear her to pieces.

The story of Bruno's ass puts the situation exactly. Bruno had an ass that he tethered exactly midway between two bales of hay. The animal starved to death.

The dilemma is therefore not a problem of deciding between yes and no, but of choosing between two equally valid *yes*'s. Whatever decision the woman makes she will be racked with guilt and shame. She cannot back off and not make a decision because that in itself would be a decision to have the baby. She must find some creative solution or she will have to find some way to rationalize one choice over the other, probably finding some way to give this choice moral superiority. What this means is the rationalization will be backed by the energy needed to reject the alternative. The energy of this rejection gives birth to morality. With this rationalization the deadlock is broken. However, the reason we brought up this dilemma again was to show that *the guilt and shame the woman feels do not come from the decision.* They were there before the decision is made. *Guilt and shame come from the schism engendered by the dilemma.*

The cry of a man in a psychiatric ward illustrates this self-generation of guilt in a heart-rending way:

> Brothers, brothers, there is immeasurable injustice. Brothers do not allow it to continue in the world. A dreadful misfortune awaits you. Brothers, I am in intolerable agony. Help, brothers, do not abandon me. I am bowed beneath the weight of excruciating guilt. I am accused of endless crime and I suffer. My situation is inextricable; I am accused on every side; I am innocent but guilty at the same time. My suffering is boundless. Can you not help me? Brothers, I am tortured, I am afraid, I am an innocent criminal.[18]

In some profound way he speaks for all humankind. We are all innocent criminals.

The original sin for which all human beings feel guilty is separation, the wound that is at the very source of our being. Me-as-center/me-as-periphery is the primordial dilemma. Both have equal weight; we cannot choose them simultaneously, but neither can we reject them, because such a rejection would destroy me as an individual. Whatever I do is wrong. Whatever I do threatens to destroy me. This is our guilt. This is our agony. It is the torture of this poor man. It is the torture of the woman with the abortion dilemma, although in her case it takes a more specific form. But even so, let her resolve this dilemma one way or the other and she will be faced with another, maybe whether to leave her husband who, because of her pregnancy, has found

---

18   Marguerite Sechehaye, trans. Grace Rubin-Rabson, *Reality Lost and Found: The Autobiography of a Schizophrenic Girl* (New York: New American Library, 1970), p. 58.

another lover. Should she stay with him and so have security and support in bringing up the baby, or should she leave and so preserve her integrity? And then there will be another dilemma, and a dilemma within a dilemma, and so on. Underlying all is the slosh and swell of the primordial dilemma and the guilt and agony accompanying it.

The third center and its concomitant, consciousness, buffer us from this agony. To help us understand better the birth of the third center by which we try to shield ourselves from this intolerable pain let us see how simpler organisms than the human being deal with this basic wound. This will call for another detour, but in the long run it will be the quickest way to go.

Territory

Have you ever noticed the neighbor's dog will run after you barking—but only so far? Here it will become hesitant, maybe yap once or twice, and then with a final look in your direction trot off home. If, when the dog started yapping and becoming hesitant, you were to make a sudden noise or movement at it, the dog would probably tuck its tail between its legs and beat an undignified retreat. We can understand Fido if we understand territory. It now seems certain all animals are territorial. That is, they have a certain space that is made possible by having a center. The nearer to the center an animal is the more psychological strength it has. Fido reaches the limit of its strength when it chases after you. At that limit it becomes hesitant, and a simple "Boo!" will be enough to scare it away.

Even some fish have territory. A type of fish called the stickleback was studied by an ethologist, who observed that a male would chase another male for a certain distance, then suddenly the tables would be reversed and the one being chased would become the pursuer. This would continue back and forth for a while, with the distance of pursuit being steadily reduced until the two fish would stand glaring at one another across an invisible barrier. Then again, suddenly, both would up-end and dive to

103

the bottom of the water and engage in activity typical of nest building.

What happens in this dance is the following: one stickleback, because it is nearer to the center, has more psychological strength than its opponent and so chases it. The opponent will withdraw to its own center and gain in strength while the pursuer, reciprocally, gets farther away from his center and loses strength. There comes a point where the pursued becomes stronger than the pursuer, hence the reversal. This continues until the strength of each is equal. Now they can neither advance nor retreat, but they cannot stay where they are. That is the dilemma. Each is poised exactly at the point of me-as-center/me-as-periphery being in equilibrium. Now tension builds to such a degree that each up-ends, dives to the bottom, and goes through the motions of nest building, which is something entirely unrelated to the confrontation.

Displacement Activity

The up-ending is a creative resolution of the tension. Ethologists' name for it is *displacement activity*. Whereas the nest-building surrogate is a creative solution, sometimes the displacement activity is destructive. For example, some male deer, instead of attacking the opponent, attack the trees in the opponent's territory. It often happens in the business world that a manager, instead of directly attacking another manager will attack by undermining one or other of the systems for which his adversary is responsible. The witch sticking pins in the wax figure of her enemy is engaged in displacement activity.

Displacement is most often creative, however, and in a way all the myriad living forms are nature's way of using it to resolve the underlying dilemma of me-as-center/me-as-periphery. Within this context we can say that consciousness is displacement activity, the human resolution of this dilemma. The focal point of consciousness and that which makes it possible is "I-it."

104

What Is Meant by I-It

There is a difference between "I" and "me." "Me" is common to all life, it is the viewpoint that makes sentience possible. With each "me" there is a world. There are countless worlds of all sizes, kinds, and potentialities: the world of the flea, the ant, the elephant, the whale, the mouse, and the moose. Each of these worlds has one center: me. The human world center is "I." "I" is articulate, connected with all experience that is either conscious or potentially conscious. Me, on the other hand, is inarticulate. It is witness, the knowing viewpoint. The animal does not "think" me; that is neither possible nor necessary, because me is inarticulate. Thinking, that is articulating, is necessary for "I." Thinking "I" is essential to the birth of "I."

As me-as-center, "I" is mine; as me-as-periphery it is not mine, and we refer to "it" not "I." As me-as-periphery, "it" is to be attained; as me-as-center "I" cannot be attained. (How does one attain that which one already is?) Now we can understand the paradox that Mircea Eliade posed when he spoke of the center that is immediately attained and always present, but which we have to make great efforts to reach. It is the center I-it. As "I" it is present. As "it" I has to be attained.

We have expressions, "Finally I am getting somewhere," or "I am not getting anywhere," or "I am going in circles," and so on. Some people carry this idea of "getting somewhere" quite far and look on life as a journey. A music hall artist at the beginning of the century used to sing these words:

> Keep right on to the end of the road;
> Keep right on to the end.
> Though you're tired and weary,
> Still carry on
> 'Til you come to your happy abode.
> All you love and you're dreaming of
> Will be there, at the end of the road.

"All you love and you're dreaming of" is I-it, the final consummation, complete realization of "I" as "it," "it" as "I." This happens at the end of the road when there is no longer any striving onward. Getting somewhere in life is getting to the center, getting home. All journeys, even the most mundane, are forms of pilgrimage. But the journey of life is an unending pilgrimage.

We talk about the rat race, the treadmill of life. We have a constant feeling of being under pressure, of having something we must do or accomplish. We feel a sense of weariness and stress. Many people want time to pass quickly. They live in constant expectation that fulfillment and true happiness will come, and therefore all that happens meanwhile is just filling in time until that happy day. I-it is the promised land, the fixed, stable, and unambiguous center that will be there at the end of the road. All our arts and sciences, philosophies, and religions aim at finding perfect equilibrium, a perfect equilibrium that evades us always.

The Three Strategies

Three strategies are available in relation to this promised center, three ways by which we try to fuse I-it and so bring an end to the torment of tomorrow: I can *be* it, *know* it, or *own* it.

Power

The strategy of *being* the center is the strategy of *power* by which the tension is overcome through domination. All manifestations of conflict, both internal and external are overcome by force. This is the iron man or iron lady solution. Hitler claimed to be the center. He said, "I am Germany; Germany is me." It is the claim made by kings, emperors, rulers, and presidents the world over. But the stronger the claim, the more suspicious, distrustful, and even paranoiac the person becomes because, in his heart, he knows he is not really the center, or, it would be better to say, he both knows that he is and knows that he is not.

Prestige

The strategy of *knowing* the center is the strategy of prestige. This is the claim to be at the pinnacle of the hierarchy. To know the center is to be privy to the secret of life. Popes, priests, and hierophants all make this claim, and with it the claim of infallibility. To know the center also means to be near or to have been near the center. This is where the pilgrimages, relics, autographs have their value. Simply to have spoken to the king could once give a subject great status among his peers. But this strategy too has its Achilles heel, because others too can claim to know the center. This is the source of jealousy and envy and, in the end, of holy wars and ideological conflicts.

Possessions

The final strategy is to *own* the center: "my" God, "my" country, "my" flag, "my" Führer, "my" house, "my" whatever. Between what is mine and me there is no distinction. A story in the newspaper, purported to be a true one, told of a cyclist in France who accidentally bumped a car. The owner of the car got out, walked to the bicycle, and without saying a word kicked the bike. The cyclist, also without saying a word, got off the bike, walked to the car, and kicked the car. The motorist, then, and still without speaking, jumped on the wheel of the bike and buckled it. Upon which the cyclist, in silence, methodically destroyed the windshield. So it continued, each destroying the other's property in silence.

To damage my property is to damage me. To desecrate the flag is to desecrate me. A person who owns a great deal is so much more vulnerable than one who owns little. Many are the people who on losing what they own lose the will to live and commit suicide.

These three strategies, power, prestige, and possessions, are ways of trying to reconcile I-it and of finally bringing the center into consciousness: to know both I and it simultaneously and unequivocally. Of course all three are used by all people to a greater or lesser degree. Power, prestige, and possessions are, according to the late Karen Horney, a celebrated psychotherapist of her day, the needs out of which the personality has developed. But the basic need is for a center, and power, prestige, and possession are but the strategies by which the center is established. They form what we could call social life.

Even so, within these strategies there is ambiguity. For example, in being the center I am such either by my own power or because others choose me as the center. I know the center either as the center of a world of truth, beauty or goodness, or through knowing the center that is outside. I own the center as my exclusive property or a property that is shared.

In addition, we have what we like to call our spiritual life. This too is devoted to the establishment of a center, one that we know as the true, the good, and the beautiful. Lastly, we have the body, which is a natural center, a center that we must protect, feed, and ensure avoids pain and gains pleasure. To explore fully the implications of this would take us too far afield and we could get lost without having added too much to our understanding of practice. But out of interest let us show the three levels in a diagram to help bring them together in your mind.

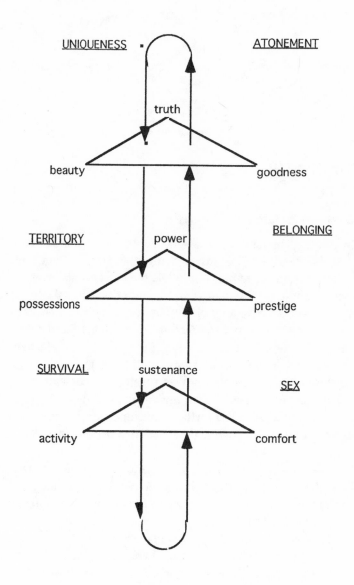

UNIQUENESS · ATONEMENT

truth

beauty goodness

TERRITORY power BELONGING

possessions prestige

SURVIVAL sustenance SEX

activity comfort

Chapter 7
You and I

Love and Hate

In the last chapter, when talking about the encounter with the neighbor, we said that extreme anger and aggression build up and will continue to build up while the combatants' eyes remain locked. Some readers will want to query this and ask, "But what about lovers? They can look into each other's eyes and, far from there being anger and aggression, there is love and adoration instead. How would you account for this?" Karen Horney said that belonging to groups and associations is just as important a need for us as the need for power, prestige, or possessions. There are also many stories of men and women sentenced to solitary confinement, who risked further punishment and even death simply to communicate with others. Other people then, far from being hell, are heaven.

That is true, and we will now spend some time talking about love, the other half of the picture. As we will see, this is half of yet another ambiguity of love and hate that we also will explore in greater depth.

It is well known that passionate love can turn to equally passionate hate and vice versa. There is, for example, what is called the Stockholm effect when a hostage falls in love with her or his abductor. The trauma of falling out of love, the impassioned hatred, malice, and destructiveness so many people have encountered when a love affair goes sour, is too well known to need any further comment. In psychoanalysis, a flip-flop from feeling positive to feeling negative about the therapist happens quite often. There is a well-known phenomenon called positive transference, when the client falls in love with the analyst. It is called "positive" to distinguish it from its opposite, negative transference, in which the analyst becomes the object of hatred. It can also happen that love and hate are inextricably bound together. An extreme example of this is the battered wife syndrome.

As long as we believe it is the other person who is responsible for the love or hate we feel, we will never be able truly to understand either emotion. But the idea that we simply project our feelings on others is very naive. This naiveté becomes obvious if we consider mystical love, or the mystic's encounter with the hellish realm. In both, the mystic-as-an-ego vanishes, in the first case through mystical union, and in the second through engulfment. So nothing remains to make the projection; there is no ego to project feelings and therefore there can be no projection.

Libido and the Dam

It is well known that mystics often use the language of love to describe their mystical experience. This is true in the Christian, Jewish, Sufi, and Hindu traditions. As a rule, commentators explain it in the following way. The mystic denies himself or herself sexual love, and so a "force" or energy is dammed up, much in the same way that a flowing river can be dammed up. Because the pressure continues to build, the mystic has to find some outlet and so resorts to imagination, and when the person is a Christian, has Christ as a lover in imagination.

Commentators explain not only love but aggression too in this way. Again, a type of energy called libido is dammed; this time, after enough pressure has built up, the dam breaks and aggression, anger, and hostility erupt. This libido theory is the basis of Freudian, Reichian, and Jungian theories and their offshoots.

The libido theory is often accompanied by the belief that a human being is simply a complex animal, and because animals are, as it is said, ruled by instincts, the human being must also be ruled by them. It is claimed that there are instincts of aggression, of sex, of love, and so on, and they use libido energy. Questions as to where this energy is stored, how it is generated, how it is dammed up, why it has a variety of characteristics such as aggression, sex, love, hate, and so on, are ignored.

In ancient times it was believed that fire came from a substance called phlogiston. Later research produced a much simpler way to explain fire. Light waves, radio waves, X rays, and so on were thought to be waves in a medium called the ether; the theory of relativity gave a simpler explanation. Just as scientists found it unnecessary to use the ideas of phlogiston and ether waves, so it is unnecessary to have the theory of instincts to explain aggression and love; nor is it necessary to believe in a life force or libido that can be dammed up or transmuted. Instead, aggression and love can both be understood within the context we have developed. We have shown to some extent how this is possible for aggression, and will now show how love can be accounted for within the same context. Furthermore, in the next chapter we will show that love and hate have exactly the same elements, me-as-center/me-as-periphery, the difference between them simply being one of emphasis.

In this chapter we concentrate mainly on love, to show that mystical love is not a sublimation of sexuality, but both are equally valid and have a common origin. It will be shown furthermore that it is not possible to draw a hard and fast line between them and say, "This is where one begins and the other ends."

Let me quote a beautiful example of mystical love. It is called "The Living Flame of Love," and is subtitled "Songs of the Soul in Intimate Union with God." It was written by St. John of the Cross, a Spanish mystic of the sixteenth century.

> O living flame of love,
> How tenderly you wound
> And sear my soul's most inward center!
> No longer so elusive,
> Now, if you will, conclude
> And rend the veil from this most sweet encounter.
> O cautery that heals!
> O consuming wound!
> O soothing hand! O touch so fine and light
> That savours of eternity
> And satisfies all dues!
> Slaying, you have converted death to life.[1]

We will comment on this poem at length at the end of the next chapter. For the present, just let us say that if we did not know who the poet was, except for the subtitle it would be impossible to say, just by reading the poem, whether the poet was talking about love inspired by a woman or by God. This is true of other examples that we will quote, some of which have a very erotic tone.

One well-known example of this eroticism is the Song of Songs of the Old Testament. Is this extolling heavenly or erotic love?

> Let him kiss me with kisses of his mouth;
> For thy love is better than wine . . .
> I was asleep, but my heart waked:
> It is the voice of my beloved that knocketh saying
> Open to me my sister, my love, my dove,
> My undefiled

---

1   Gerald Brennar, *St. John of the Cross* (Cambridge: Cambridge University Press), p. 163.

For my head is filled with dew
My locks with the drops of the night.[2]

Or consider these lines from a poem celebrating the love of a Gopi girl, Radha, for Krishna. Krishna is highly revered as a god in India, and ancient Hindu texts say that long ago he came to earth, bringing with him all the people and things of his heaven, and all that happens eternally in heaven was enacted, in time, on earth.

> He was infatuated, she bewildered;
> he was clever, and she naive.
>
> He put out his hand to touch her; she quickly pushed it away.
> He looked into her face, her eyes filled with tears.
>
> He held her forcefully, she trembled violently
> and hid her face from his kisses behind the edge of her sari.
>
> Then she lay down, frightened, beautiful as a doll;
> he hovered like a bee round a lotus in a painting.[3]

We can compare these mystical poems to the words of a song made popular in the 1940s by movie star Nelson Eddy:

> You are my heart's delight
> And where you are
> I long to be.
> You make my darkness bright
> and like a star
> you shine on me.

Is this a song of divine love or of erotic love? Who is this "you" who "are my heart's delight"?

---

2   Song of Songs 1:2, 5:2.

3   Edward C. Dimock, Jr., and Denise Levertov, trans., *In Praise of Krishna* (New York: Anchor Books, 1967), p. 11.

Who Are You?

Nelson Eddy, we would probably say, was singing to an ideal woman. If a woman had sung the song, it would have been some ideal man. Although it is not out of the question that St. John wrote his poem with a woman in mind, in view of the subtitle, most people believe that the beloved is Christ or God. But is this Christ an ideal or a transcendent reality? The beloved in the Krishna poem is Krishna, but again the same question arises: Does that mean Krishna an ideal, or Krishna a transcendent reality.

By "transcendent reality" we mean a reality that has no form but even so is real. On the other hand, by "ideal" man or woman we mean an *idea* of a perfect person. The difference between the ideal and the real is something like the difference between the menu and the meal. If it is a transcendent reality that is in question, are Christ and Krishna two different transcendent realities, or one transcendent reality interpreted in two different ways? Furthermore, where are these realities, how do they exist.

Moreover, if we claim transcendent reality for Christ or Krishna, why should we not say that the "you" of the popular song is also transcendent? To deny this would seem arbitrary. Is it possible, therefore, all three are the *same you*, and, moreover, a you that is real but transcendent, a "you" encountered in many, many different ways? Let us remember there are millions of references to this "you" in poems, songs, stories, films, prayers, scriptures, rituals, and ceremonies. Is there a "you" common to them all? If so who is this "you?"

Earlier we spoke of Plato's myth, which tells of the time when we were whole and the gods out of fear and jealousy cut us in two. According to the myth we have since had to wander forever seeking our other half. Plato says, "It is really the burning longing for unity which bears the name of love." Could it be that through the mystical *you* or the erotic *you* we are seeking our original wholeness?

The Search

Mystical poetry clearly shows there *is* truly such a search. For example, in another poem St. John writes,

> Where have you hidden away
> Beloved, and left me here to mourn?
> Having wounded me you fled
> Like the hart: I followed on
> Behind you, crying out, calling—and you were gone.[4]

"Songs in Praise of Krishna" also contains a poem that includes these lines:

> When they had made love
> she lay in his arms in the kunja grove.
> Suddenly she called his name
> and wept—as if she burned in the fire of separation.
> The gold was in her ornament
> but she looked for it afar!
> —Where has he gone? Where has my love gone?
> O why has he left me alone?
> And she writhed on the ground in despair,
> only her pain kept her from fainting.
> Krishna was astonished and could not speak.[5]

In the Song of Songs it says.

> By night on my bed I sought him whom my soul loveth
> I sought him, but I found him not.
> I said, I will rise now and go about the city
> In the streets and in the broad ways
> I will seek him whom my soul loveth
> I sought him but found him not.[6]

---

4   Brennar, *St. John of the Cross,* p. 149.

5   Dimock and Levertov, *In Praise of Krishna,* p. 23.

These three examples leave no doubt that a search arises from the longing for "you who are my heart's delight." In the third quotation the words "sought" and "seek" are used four times in almost as many lines.

Something else in the last two quotations must be stressed because it is a vital clue if we wish to understand mystical and profane love. The Song of Songs (2:16) says "My beloved is mine and I am his." *Then immediately afterward* (3:1) *it says*, "I sought him but found him not."

In the Radha poem the poet even inserts the comment "the gold was in her ornament but she looked for it afar!"

These two quotations are reminiscent of a story that Yasutani roshi used to tell. Enyadatta was a beautiful girl who would often look at herself in the mirror. One day she looked and found her head was no longer there. She was so upset that she ran everywhere looking for it. All her friends tried to persuade her she was mistaken, saying it was not possible such an important part of herself could be separated from her and lost. One day someone gave her a sharp crack on the head. "There," he said, "that is your head!" And with that Enyadatta realized she was whole and complete and that she had never been otherwise.

Enyadatta loses her head, Radha loses the beloved. Both are expressions of the same mistaken belief that we all share that we can lose the Other. But, as we have often said, Buddhism teaches that we are whole and complete just as we are, so how can we lose half of ourselves? We are whole and complete, One, and the gods can only cut us in half with our consent.

According to a Christian saying, "If you had not already found me you would not be seeking me." This sums up the situation well enough. But even so, the truth may be deeper yet: We seek the Other not simply because we have *found* the Other, but because

---

6   3:1.

117

we *are* the Other. *Wholeness includes Otherness.* And not only this. We must go further yet and say, "Because you have found me, because you are whole, you *have* to seek me." *It is because we are whole and complete that we have to suffer.*

Let us see if we can unpack that and say more clearly what it means.

I-Thou

Another way of saying wholeness includes otherness is, "You and I" are not separate, both emerge from a common ground, both emerge simultaneously and are interdependent. Furthermore you are constant, but you take on many forms. You are my wife, my child, my boss, my enemy, my God, and my devil. Try this for yourself. Think of all kinds of people and for each say "you." The same you is applied to all; by this is not meant the same *word* you, but the same distinctive *feeling* of "you." When the distinctions arise, "you" has become "him" or "her," Judy, Jim, or Jane.

Just as we have seen the trinity of Oneness and the trinity of awareness, so there is a trinity of "I." We have already encountered two of these: the one we have called "me" and the one we have called I-it. Now we have the third, which could be called I-Thou. The words are joined, implying there can be no separation of I from Thou or I from You.

If you are familiar with the writings of Martin Buber, the Jewish philosopher, you will already be familiar with the terms I-Thou and I-it. He said both are *primary words,* and there is no "I" on its own. He said that it is only with the whole of our being that we can speak the primary word I-Thou, but we can never speak I-it in that way. Furthermore, when I-Thou is spoken, nothing is involved, whereas I-it always involves something.

Much is common between what Buber said and what we are saying here. To say that we can only speak I-Thou with one's whole being is to say that I-Thou *is* the whole. No I exists on its own because I is a part of the whole. Furthermore, we can never speak I-it with our whole being because I-it is a flight from the tension that comes from the ambiguity inherent in I-Thou. When I-Thou is spoken, nothing is involved because existence has yet to emerge. I-Thou is upstream of existence. But, it is precisely when I-it comes into being that something comes into being.

However, there is a difference in what we are saying and what Buber says: I-Thou is ambiguous and not simply a compound word. It is ambiguous just as "me" and I-it are. Let us explore this question of the three "I's" a little more deeply.

First, we are not saying there are three distinct "I's" any more than we said there were three distinct Ones. Nor are we even saying that we can make a sharp distinction among "I," Oneness, and Awareness. Using the analogy often given by Buddha, we can say that although we can speak of milk, cheese, yogurt, and butter, there is only one substance. So we can speak of Awareness, Oneness, and "I" and yet they are not substantially different. The distinction among them arises out of our naming, and we name to capture qualities even though in the nameless there is no distinction. Words are not unlike a prism that, when pure, colorless light passes through it, breaks this light down into many different colors. "I," Oneness, and Awareness are refractions of the light of the world passed through the prism of words.

The ambiguity of me-as-center/me-as-periphery is never resolved, but with the use of words the tension and dynamism arising out of this ambiguity are transmuted into *objectivity*. However, because of this transmutation, objects come to have a lifeless, eternal quality. They exist, that is, stand out, for us through the names we give them. One of the functions of a painter or a poet is to penetrate the veil of words and concepts and so restore life to the world. It is of some interest that the letter, the smallest unit of language, was called by the ancient Indian philosophers in Sanskrit *aksara*, which meant "stable," "durable," whereas the "word" was called *vac*, associated with God and eternity. The dead, lifeless quality imparted by words is epitomized in legal documents, in which the writer uses great care to define words clearly and apply them unambiguously. That deadening, objectifying capacity is also evident with stereotyping in which words are used to reduce others to objects. For example, yid, frog, limey, slopes, and so on, all make objects of the beings referred to. The dynamic, living tension of the ambiguous I-Thou is thereby objectified and destroyed, and by this the inherent threat is apparently eliminated.

Let us look closer at this inherent threat. As we know, me-as-center/me-as-periphery is irreducible. It is this irreducible quality that gives rise to the feeling of the alien. In the presence of the Other there is a characteristic feel, which is just that: the feeling of a *presence*. Now it is quite possible to have this feeling of presence without another *person* being present. In the next chapter we give a striking example of what we mean by this *presence without another person being present*. However, we are all familiar with it. We all know that eerie, alien feeling that can come on us when we are alone in a house, especially in the dark, of another being in the room. We also know this feeling can become strong enough to create anxiety, even panic. Buddha knew this fear and once said, "I spend then those nights in shrines of forest, park, or tree, fearsome and hair-raising as they are, making such shrines my lodging for the night, that I may behold for myself the panic, fear and horror of it all."[7]

This alien quality is not simply fearful. It is also the basis of the erotic. It is the otherness of the feminine that, for a man, is a basic ingredient in the erotic quality of a woman. This otherness is enhanced by the taboo zones of a woman's genitals, breasts, legs, and, in some cultures, face. A woman writing of the erotic said:

---

7 Woodward, *Some Sayings of the Buddha*, pp. 14-15.

But that is the dilemma. If there's no "other" anymore, desire dies. Wanting to encounter the strangerwanting to keep everything familiar. The contradictory needs between which passion falters! We try to get around the conflict by keeping both needs apart: Sleepy domestic security, fatal attraction to the stranger.[8]

But these two, which we are naming I-Thou and that earlier we called me-as-center/me-as-periphery, are not only irreconcilable, they are also interdependent, sharing a common ground. *"Me" is this common ground that gives the feeling of intimacy.* It too is the basis of the erotic, this time of the homo-erotic. This same writer speaks of the lesbian encounter:

In each of my relationships with women . . . there was an exhilarating sense of oneness, belonging, sacred marriage, yes. But, at the same time, with our ideal of sameness, we kept each other from our otherness. . . . We made the other into ourselves.[9]

"You" emerge out of this quality of the alien and the intimate, of wanting to encounter the strange, wanting to keep everything familiar. You are different from me. In your difference is my pain or fear. You and I are *one* and in our no-difference is my pleasure. I yearn for you "who are my heart's delight" in whom there is no alienness, no Otherness. But, as the author points out, I can only do this *because* you are alien, *because* you are Other.

You as a concrete person crystallize out of this mixture of the intimate and the alien. You are different from me, and ultimately, when the common ground is lost, this difference becomes

---

8   Kim Chernin and Renate Stendhal, *Sex and Other Sacred Games* (New York: Fawcett Columbine, 1990), p. 236.

9   *Ibid.*

separation and is painful. But when the intimate balances the alien, then there is pleasure and relaxation. The art of the erotic is to walk the tightrope between intimacy and alien, a tightrope that many find easier to walk by having the intimacy of wife on the one hand and the alien of the lover on the other.

In daily life we experience the pain and fear generated by the Other mostly just as tension. Take, for example, the argument with the neighbor, and let us forgo for the moment a creative solution to the problem through compromise and discussion. Even just anticipating the meeting can make one tense. One feels rigid in the neck and shoulders, knotted in the stomach. This tension is the physical counterpart of the irreconcilability yet unity of me-as-center/me-as-periphery. If one were to ask why we are tense we might say something like, "I can imagine what he is going to say." However, imagination, no less than the actual encounter, merely acts as the trigger, the explosives are already packed in the unresolvable ambiguity.

Uncountable numbers of situations can create just that tension: taking an exam, visiting the doctor, flying in an airplane, and so on. If we observe these situations carefully we see that in each we are trying to establish a certainty where no certainty is possible. The worst type of tension arises when two completely contradictory outcomes exist, both equally desirable but only one of which is possible and neither of which can give way.

We want, for example, to have friendly and open relations with the neighbor, maybe even, at a deeper level, we would like the neighbor to see us as a loving, kind person. This want comes out of the common ground we share. But, we *also* want our own way. Both are whole resolutions: with the first, as a loving and kind person we could conceivably agree with the neighbor completely, give him what he wants, and so restore harmony and goodwill. Or, with the second, we could control the neighbor completely, and get him to do everything we want. So again we get rid of conflict and restore harmony. But each of these resolutions vies with the other; neither gives way.

However, this conflict with the neighbor is simply a personification of the irreconcilable conflict within me. The search for certainty is the search to resolve the dilemma that underlies this and all similar confrontations and conflicts. *But, this very search for certainty in its turn creates suffering, because by searching we turn our backs on our own intrinsic wholeness. It is because we are whole that we seek to restore wholeness. Through this search, through the need for certainty, we destroy wholeness, and the tension arises.*

The Evil Eye

Let us see if we can clarify further the connection between me-as-center/me-as-periphery, between I and Thou, between me and the neighbor.

We have said it is the presence of the Other that makes one tense, and that the Other need not have the form of another person, for example, of the neighbor. If we are attentive, we will see that the eerie quality of the presence of the Other is the feeling that we are being observed. There is, it is felt, another awareness that is aware of me. When another is present as a concrete person it is possible for us to say, "Yes, this awareness is hers, or his. She or he is aware of me." But is it really her or his awareness that I experience? Is the awareness that I feel when you are there your awareness of me, or do you simply awaken me to this awareness? Do you simply give this awareness focus?

When we talked about eye contact in our argument with the neighbor we mentioned the tension that could build up because of it. This same tension can build up in a young child alone in bed in the dark. There is a sudden rise of panic and the child screams in terror. If we ask what is the matter, the child might well say, "There's a bogey man under my bed." It is the bogey man that terrifies the child. The bogey man terrifies by being aware of the child. We look under the bed but no one is there. We say, "It's just your imagination. Go to sleep." But it is not just imagination, although, admittedly, it is not the bogey man. *It is an awareness of.* The child is aware of this awareness of the child. Put differently, it is an awareness of awareness of awareness of . . . in a vicious circle that threatens to engulf the child and that creates the panic. Your physical presence breaks this vicious circle.

That eye contact has this potential is well known, and society has developed various mechanisms to minimize the tension. For example, it is bad manners to stare at someone. Keeping the eyes lowered is a way of showing respect for another. Furthermore, even when you are with a friend you will find you will meet his or her eyes and then look away and then meet and look away and so on. People in power often demand that those over whom they have power keep the eyes down. Anyone who has been in boot camp knows the relish with which sergeants shout, "Don't you eyeball me, soldier! Keep your eyes down!" In certain parts of most big cities it is good policy to avoid eye contact as much as possible, as this will lessen the likelihood of a confrontation.

The potential of eye contact to create tension, and therefore, anxiety and fear, is sometimes exploited. Some Buddhist temples have guardians, statues equipped with glaring eyes. These statues also have a ferocious attitude, but the real menace is in the eyes. Some butterflies, insects, and fish use staring eyes as a form of camouflage. These are not real eyes but natural markings on the wings of butterflies, or on the bodies of caterpillars and fish. Such staring eyes, whether they originate from nature or a sculptor, are a form of protection.

I remember in my childhood being terrified by a nearby church. It had a tall, pointed steeple and four clock faces that lit up at night, two of them facing my bedroom window. In the twilight the church looked like some huge demonic wizard in a conical hat. But the real terror came from those two malevolent unblinking eyes.

Or did it? There was nothing inherently terrible in the clock faces. I was not being looked at. What the clock faces did was the same as what the markings on the butterfly wings do. They awakened the basic wound. By the very act of looking, I *was looked at*. It is not that I look, see the clock faces, and realize the clock faces are like eyes looking at me, but *being seen is inherent in seeing*.

One sometimes gets faint echoes of this when going into a hotel room. There is a feeling of malevolence, of being looked at. Film directors exploit this feeling in movies when they allow the camera to play, for just a fraction too long, on what is otherwise an innocuous object. It is like looking into a mirror and no longer being sure which is the reality and which the reflection.

German mystic Meister Eckhart said, "The eye with which I see God is the eye with which God sees me." We could just as well say, "The eye with which I see the hotel room is the eye with which the hotel room sees me." This eye is simply given form, even though it may be the stylized form of two round clock faces. It, not the clock faces, has the power to swallow and so be swallowed.

This too is the basis of the fear of the dark. In the dark one has no familiar objects to provide a center, and therefore seeing the darkness is being seen by it. It is also the basis for the fear of being in a house alone. Again, one has no center that lends itself readily and so the basic ambiguity begins to assert itself. In some cultures people create shrines or altars in their houses to provide a center and so lessen the fear of being alone.

People with mental illness may have just this problem of not being able to establish a center.[10] They may therefore fear that they are being looked at and observed, or that people are plotting against them. This is known as paranoia. It is not surprising that staring eyes are the subject of some psychotic art.

What we have said helps us understand why human relations can be so complex. Each relationship involves four people: me,

---

10   Low, *The Iron Cow of Zen*, pp. 86-89.

the one looked at; me, the one looking; she, the one looked at; and she, the one looking. Each can be the focus of a personality completely different from the others. One could work out permutations in which each of these personalities likes or dislikes the other, and from this build up a scenario as dramatic, or as comic, as any that theater has known.

Freud wrote in one of his letters, "I am accustoming myself to the idea of regarding every sexual act as a process in which four persons are involved." Rebecca Goldstein explores this idea to some extent:

> In gazing with desire on the Other I reveal how he, in my desire, takes me over, permeates my sense of self; and in his gaze I see how I similarly matter to him, who himself matters at that moment so much. It is this double reciprocal process that accounts, I think, for the psychological intensity of sexual experience.[11]

She looks at me and I see I matter to her. While this is happening I am also looking at her and so she sees she matters to me (who, as we have said, is seeing me matter to her.) This double reciprocal process is again the feedback, the microphone/loudspeaker syndrome. She, however, is secondary. Primary to this double reciprocal process is me-as-center/me-as-periphery. That she is secondary becomes evident when we consider the mystic's experience. Radha says:

> From the time our eyes first met
> our longing grew.
> He was not only the desirer, I not only the desired
> passion ground our hearts together in its mortar.[12]

---

11   Rebecca Goldstein, *The Mind Body Problem* (Davenport, Fla.: Laura Books, 1983), p. 212.

12   Dimock and Levertov, *In Praise of Krishna*, p. 41.

He was not only the desirer, he was also the desired. I was not only the desired, I was also the desirer. For him I was the trigger. For me he was the trigger, the trigger that released the tension between the desirer and the desired, both of which are me. To say she or he is secondary does not mean the mystic's encounter is imaginary. It is prior to imagination, prior to experience even. The mystic's encounter arises at the very source of reality. Truly it is this encounter that makes all encounters possible. But it is not the encounter of *someone* with *someone*.

Otherness is inherent in wholeness. The less form we give to the Other, the more we are one with it, the greater love we have and the greater potential we have to realize the Other as ourselves, ourselves as the Other. This is why we said I-Thou is upstream of existence. We can understand why, in an old popular song, one lover talks about the other as stepping out of a dream:

> You stepped out of a dream,
> You are too wonderful
> To be what you seem . . .

In a dream the Other is oneself, the self is the Other. But in this dream state can also lurk evil. In the erotic there is also evil; why else would it be so condemned by so many religions? Aleister Crowley, an Englishman who lived at the beginning of this century, claimed to be a black magician and tried to exploit this evil in the erotic by combining sexuality and magic. Satanic masses and erotic orgies are often found together, and the forbidden is one of the more exquisite aspects of the sexual experience. The collapse of the erotic into the terrible scourge of rape and serial murder is well known when the Thou is transformed into an it. Heaven and hell are not two domains. In the one is the other.

In the next chapter we will sum up where we have got to, giving a map of the territory we have traversed so far. Then we will try to penetrate a little more deeply into the question of how it is possible that, in one glance, there is heaven as well as hell.

127

Chapter 8
Heaven and Hell

In this chapter we would like to give some support to what we have said so far, in the form of mystical experiences that people have had. Four of them are positive experiences of heavenly states, and the fifth is a negative experience of a hellish state. We will analyze them to show how they illustrate what we have said thus far. This will give the opportunity, as we promised in the previous chapter, to show exactly how the same elements are present in love and in hate, in ecstasy and in horror. We end the chapter with an analysis of St. John's poem that appears on page 112 to show how it summarizes all that we have said.

Before continuing with this, and to make it easier for you to find your way through the labyrinth of mind that we have traversed together, let me offer you a map in the form of another scale, shown on the next page.

This scale represents the involution of true nature into consciousness. We use the word involution, and not evolution, because the latter suggests progress and development. There can be no improvement and progress of true nature. Thus involution suggests entanglement and involvement, which is more descriptive.

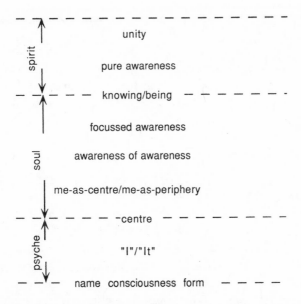

Each level of the scale is discrete and independent of the others, but nonetheless inextricably involved in all levels. To show what we mean we could use, as an analogy, another more familiar scale, the scale of matter:

subatomic particles
atoms
molecules
cells
organs
bodies

One can consider each level independent of the others, or perceive them as coexisting as a body. Similarly, the levels in the scale of awareness can be perceived either as independent or as coexisting in the everyday experiences of life.

Let us now examine in more detail the various levels of the scale of awareness.

Unity

Basic to all is unity, which, as we have shown, is not simply an abstract generalization but a vital and dynamic source of all. Unity is not simply Oneness; it is also Emptiness and a Trinity. This Trinity has affinities with the Christian Trinity of God the Father, God the Son, and God the Holy Spirit.[1]

Pure Awareness

Pure awareness is the light of the world. It is without reflection. It is the tenth person in the parable we gave in the introduction. This light is pointed to in a Zen koan that asks, "Where does the light of a candle go when it is blown out?" Again, it must be emphasized that all religions tell of this light. However, it is not a light that can be seen. A certain mystical experience involves seeing a wonderful, loving light, but this is not what we are referring to. Such a light comes and goes, but the light of the world neither comes nor goes. A Zen master said:

> The entire universe is reflected by the eye of a monk, the entire universe is contained in everyday conversation, the entire world is throughout your body, the entire world is your Divine light, the entire world is within your divine light and the entire world is inseparable from yourself.[2]

There was an emperor of China who, during a religious ceremony, saw a brilliant light shining in the hallway. He was overjoyed by the experience and told his courtiers about it. All, except

---

1   Many other religions and spiritual paths have similar primordial trinities. For example, the supernal triad of the Jewish cabbalah: *Ain, Ain Soph* and *Ain Soph Aur*; three levels of emptiness; and the three *kayas* or "bodies" of Buddha, the *sambhogakaya, dharmakaya* and *nirmanakaya*.

2   Kosen Nishiyama and John Stevens, trans., *Shobogenzo* (Tokyo: Daihokkaiku, 1975), p. 53.

one person, congratulated the emperor on his good fortune, saying that it was proof of his virtue and noble spirit. The dissenting one was a Buddhist who said to the emperor, "The light you saw was not the light of Buddha, it was only the light of the dragon which protects you." Then the emperor asked him, "Well, what is the light of the Buddha?" The courtier was silent.[3]

Being and Knowing

We said earlier we do not have to be aware of, or know, something to be, or be something to know. Our true nature is knowing that is being, being that is knowing. It is precisely the illusory separation of knowing and being that is at the root of our woe. Knowing-being is another way of saying "all is mind." But, alas, if we call it mind, knowing-being, God, Buddha, or Brahman, we freeze it and truth is lost, just as when we call it Oneness, Emptiness, and so on. That is why Zen masters are so adamant about not clinging to words. Zen master Joshu said, "If I use the word Buddha I want to wash my mouth out for three days." It was why Master Tokusan said, "All the scriptures are only the records of ghosts," and why Huang Po, whom we quoted earlier, said, "If you can only rid yourselves of conceptual thought you will have accomplished everything."

However, to begin with, we have to use words; but once we have the meaning, we must throw the words away.

The Remaining Levels

As we have already said so much about the other levels it is not necessary to discuss them now. However, let us repeat that although each level can be seen as discrete, it is only by long and arduous practice that human beings can make the separation.

---

3   *Ibid.*, p. 55.

Just as it is only by a long and laborious practice that the physicists could differentiate the various levels of matter. I see a garden. I talk to you. All levels of awareness are present in the richness of these immediate experiences, in the experience of everyday mind with all its stress and suffering, its beauty and joy.

The Spirit, the Soul, and the Psyche

One of the themes of this book has been to show there is no antagonism between Zen and Christianity. To practice Buddhism it is not necessary to burn the Bible, nor is it necessary to leave the Church in order to meditate in a Zendo. To practice Buddhism is to awaken to the truth, the truth that is free from exclusiveness and judgments of superiority and inferiority, free from ignorance.

On the scale, we suggested a comparison of levels of awareness and what Christianity calls the soul and spirit. Some may feel that this comparison is somewhat arbitrary, and to help make the point two quotations are offered in support. The British poet John Keats said that some people call the world:

> "A vale of tears" from which we are to be redeemed by a certain arbitrary interposition of God and taken to Heaven— What a little circumscribed straightened notion! Call the world if you Please "The vale of soul making." . . . I say "Soul making." Soul distinguished from an Intelligence— There may be intelligences or sparks of the divinity in millions—but they are not Souls till they acquire identities, till each one is personally itself.[4]

The spark of intelligence that Keats refers to is me, and, as we said earlier, me is common to all that is sentient. Every flea, ant, mouse, elephant, and rhinoceros is me. But identity is "I," and it is attained only by conscious labor.

---

4   John Keats, *Selected Letters* (New York: Doubleday, 1951), p. 257.

Jacob Needleman offers more support for calling this structure the soul. Part of his book is devoted to the teachings of a certain Father Sylvan. At one point Needleman says:

> In short the soul is not a fixed entity. According to Father Sylvan, it is a movement that begins whenever man experiences the pain of contradiction.[5]

He suggests the soul is an energy and says, "Whenever there is pain or contradiction this energy of the soul is released or 'activated'."[6] He also quotes one of the desert fathers on the practice that is necessary in soul creation:

> Keep your mind there in the heart, trying by every means possible to find the place where the heart is, in order that, having found it you should constantly abide there. Wrestling thus, the mind will find the place of the heart.[7]

Commenting on this Needleman says:

> With this, suddenly, I am known for what I am. I do not know the place of the heart; it is that which I must find. It is not something that I can assume. But this point is almost never made in all the literature of Christian mystics. Or rather, if it is made it is in a language and form that we modern people cannot recognize. We falsely assume we can find the place of the heart, or that we are already there. . . . [This] method of attention and prayer is meant to guide us toward the heart, the center of our being. It does not start from the heart; it leads to the heart.[8]

---

5   Jacob Needleman, *Lost Christianity* (New York: Bantam Books, 1982), p. 170.

6   *Ibid.*

7   *Ibid.*, p. 156.

8   *Ibid.*, p. 157.

However, it is not that "we falsely assume we can find the place of the heart, or that we are already there." We *can* find the place of the heart because we *are* already there. It is also true, as Needleman says, "I do not know the place of the heart, it is that which I must find." As we saw in the words of Eliade, we are at the center but we also have to make great efforts to get to the center, what Needleman calls the place of the heart.

Consciousness as Name and Form

Form is the basis for consciousness, and it is the constant promise of consciousness that the center will emerge as form. As part of this endeavor to fix the center in form we name it. But, because the center constantly eludes being captured, we can never say what we really mean and we must constantly renew our efforts of expression.

> Words strain,
> crack and sometimes break under the burden,
> Under the tension, slip slide, perish,
> Decay with imprecision, will not stay in place
> Will not stay still.[9]

Five Accounts

We pass from pure awareness, through awareness of awareness, through me-as-center/me-as-periphery, by way of a traumatic contradiction and the birth of the third center, into consciousness and experience. Can we do more than define all this? Is it possible to show this involution actually happening? We can through what are called mystical experiences. Five such experiences illustrate this involution.

---

9   Eliot, "Burnt Norton," *Four Quartets*, p. 12.

Account No. 1

The first experience is from an account given by Zen master Han Shan:

> One evening during meditation I clearly saw the Great Illuminating-Whole, pellucid, transparent, void and clear like a limpid ocean—nothing at all existed! Whereupon I uttered the following stanza:

> Clear and void shines the ocean like moonlight on the snow,
> No trace of men or gods can anywhere be found.
> When the Vajra eye is opened the mirage disappears
> And into stillness vanishes the earth.

> After this experience I returned to my room. Upon my desk lay the Surangaman Sutra. Casually I opened it and came across the following sentence:

> "You will then see both your body and mind, together with the mountains, rivers, space and earth of the outward world are all within the wonderful, illumined and true Mind."[10]

Account No. 2

Another master, Meng Shan, talks about an experience he had while working on a koan:

> When I reached this state, the feeling was like the moon in water—transparent and penetrating. Impossible to disperse or obliterate by rolling surges, it was inspiring, alive and vivid all the time.[11]

---

10   Chang Chen-chi, *The Practice of Zen* (London: Rider & Co., 1960), pp. 112-13.

11   *Ibid.*, p. 122.

Account No. 3

This account is by a Westerner who, as far as can be seen, did not practice any spiritual discipline:

> There was just the room with its shabby furniture and the fire burning in the grate and the red shaded lamp on the table. But, the room was filled by a Presence, which in a strange way was both about me and within me, like light or warmth. I was overwhelmingly possessed by Someone who was not myself, and yet I felt I was more myself than I had ever been before. I was filled with an intense happiness, and almost unbearable joy, such as I had never known before and have never known since.[12]

Account No. 4

The person who tells of the fourth experience also, although it happened while he was in church, did not follow any spiritual practice, and this was the first experience of its kind he had had:

> Upon that instant the luminous haze engulfing me and all around me became transformed into golden glory, into light untellable. . . . The golden light of which the violet haze seemed now to have been as the veil or outer fringe, welled forth from a central immense globe of brilliancy. . . . But the most wonderful thing was that these shafts and waves of light, that vast expanse of photosphere, and even the great central globe itself, were crowded to solidarity with the forms of living creatures . . . a single coherent organism filling all place and space, yet composed of an infinitude of individuated existences.[13]

---

12   E.C. Happold, *Mysticism: A Study and Anthology* (Harmondsworth: Pelican, 1963), p. 134.

13   *Ibid.*, p. 133.

We will withhold account number 5 until we have made an analysis of these first four.

Analysis of Account No. 1

This is an account of pure samadhi, that is, awareness of awareness. The awareness is thoroughly interfused because it is the first emergence from pure nonreflected awareness. Nevertheless, the account contains an incipient duality that becomes increasingly marked in the subsequent accounts as awareness involves into consciousness. An analysis of these accounts will therefore illustrate the birth of consciousness from awareness.

Han Shan speaks of "the Great Illuminating-Whole, pellucid, transparent, void and clear like a limpid ocean." This is a description of *awareness*. But the master is *aware of* this awareness. It is true that he uses the words "I clearly saw," but it is obvious he does not mean he saw with his eyes, rather that he was "aware of." Thus the duality: the Great Illuminating-Whole on the one hand, and clearly seeing this whole on the other.

Another small but revealing point has to be clarified.

He calls awareness the Great Illumina*ting*-Whole; however, were he simply referring to awareness he should have used the expression "Illumina*ted*-Whole." As we said, this is a very small point but an important one, because the Great Illuminating-Whole is illuminating something, and that something can only be the whole. The Great Illuminating-Whole is not therefore just awareness, but awareness that Illuminates. In other words it is itself already awareness of awareness. Thus out of pure undivided awareness there arises the first beginnings of a duality, a separation. Han Shan also says, "Nothing at all existed." We will return to this in a moment.

Analysis of Account No. 2

In the next account of Meng Shan there is the stirring of me-as-center/me-as-periphery. The alternation we spoke of earlier, first when talking about the picture of the faces and the

137

vase and later when talking about me-as-center/me-as-periphery, begins to be experienced like the ground swell at sea. Meng Shan also describes the experience of the clarity and transparency of awareness of awareness. He refers to it in contradictory terms as being like "the moon in water—*transparent and penetrating*" (my emphasis). "Transparent" is passive, like a window, and refers to awareness. "Penetrating" is active; it refers to awareness of. But instead of the tranquility so eloquently described in the previous account by "clear and void shines the ocean like moonlight on the snow," he speaks of the experience being "inspiring, alive and vivid all the time," and he says the experience was "impossible to disperse or obliterate by rolling surges." The rolling surges are the first stirring of alternation. We spoke of this alternation on several occasions and do not have to repeat the implications of it. But let us remember that normally these rolling surges break up the tranquility of the mind, it being precisely the tension arising out of them that eventually makes necessary the creation of the third center.

Analysis of Account No. 3

In the first account it is said, "I clearly saw the Great Illuminating-Whole." With this there is the first entry of the ambiguous and heterogeneous. In the second account this heterogeneity is more manifest as the beginning of alternation. In the third account heterogeneity becomes completely manifest, and the Other appears.

We wrote of this when we described the presence that the young child calls the bogey man and that causes adults to shiver in an empty house. This Other is the You of the mystics and "You who are my heart's delight" of lovers. This Other has been called Christ, Krishna, and God. Indeed, the person who gave this account realized just this and said, "If I say that Christ came to me I should be using conventional words which would carry no precise meaning; for Christ comes to men and women in different ways. When I tried to record the experience at the time

138

I used the imagery of the vision of the Holy Grail; it seemed to me to be like that."[14] But this other, this Presence, is the other half lopped off by the gods in Plato's myth; it is the other half of me.

The Other is a presence that "was about me and within me." "The presence was about me" refers to me-as-periphery. "The presence was within me" refers to me-as-center. "I was possessed by someone not myself" also refers to me-as-periphery. Yet "I was more myself than I had ever been before" refers again to the expression of me-as-center. However, we must remember that me-as-center/me-as-periphery cannot be split in this fashion, and the experience is one seamless whole. The unbearable joy, the intense happiness, comes as each aspect supports and reinforces the other.

Analysis of Account No. 4

Here the center becomes more pronounced, and therefore this account could be looked on as describing the stage just before its emergence as the third center. If we were to describe the first account as awareness of, the second and third accounts become increasingly awareness of awareness of awareness of.... A center of awareness, which is also a center of which awareness is aware, is crystallizing out in a vortex of self-reflection. In this account the crystallization is expressed by "welled forth from a central immense globe of brilliancy." Again, there is the illumination, but now instead of the coolness and vastness of the moonlight of Meng Shan, it is the intensity and vitality of sunlight: "golden glory, light untellable."

Notice the words "engulfing me." Earlier we saw that this expression of engulfment was the expression of horror and terror. It is now an expression of joy. This account gives the description

---

14   *Ibid.*, p. 133.

139

of two centers dancing around each other, or of center becoming periphery and periphery becoming center. In becoming center there is heightened awareness, energy, and joy; in becoming periphery there is heightened space, freedom, and peace. Yet there are not two wholes but just a single coherent whole, a single coherent organism filling all place and space. In Radha's poem center and periphery merge in a single globe of brilliancy:

> From the time our eyes first met
> our longing grew.
> He was not only the desirer, I not only the desired;
> passion ground our hearts together in its mortar.[15]

Account No. 5—Heaven and Hell: Not One—Not Two

We have already quoted this account, but here it is in full:

> Suddenly, I was aware that all life around me had come to a complete standstill. Everywhere I looked, instead of life, I saw a hideous nothingness invading and strangling the life out of every object and vista in sight. It was a world being choked to death by an insidious void, whereby every remaining movement was but the final throes of death. The sudden withdrawal of life left in its wake a scene of death, dying and decay so monstrous and terrible to look upon I thought to myself: no man can see this and live! My body froze to the spot.
>
> The immediate reaction was to ward off the view, to make the vision go away by finding some explanation or meaning for it; in a word, to rationalize it away. Just as I reached for each defense, the knowledge that I had not a single weapon dawned in me like a sudden blow to the head, and in the same instant I understood this thing called self; it is man's defense against seeing absolute nothingness, against seeing

---

15 Dimock and Levertov, *In Praise of Krishna*, p. 41.

a world devoid of life, a world devoid of God. Without a self, a man is defenseless against such a vision, a vision he cannot possibly live with.[16]

Contrast this with:

The most wonderful thing was that these shafts and waves of light, that vast expanse of photosphere, and even the great central globe itself, were crowded to solidarity with the forms of living creatures . . . a single coherent organism filling all place and space, yet composed of an infinitude of individuated existences.[17]

The first account said, "Nothing at all existed!" But this "nothing at all" was accompanied with wonder and joy. This fifth account says, "In the same instant I understood this thing called self; it is man's defense against seeing absolute nothingness..

It also says, "The immediate reaction was to ward off the view, to make the vision go away by finding some explanation or meaning for it; in a word, to rationalize it away." This person wanted to find some way to integrate what was happening with the rest of her experience, to tie it down with words and thoughts and so use the barrier of consciousness as protection.

This account too is of awareness of awareness of. . . . Instead of a dance of centers each yielding to the other, now each wishes to dominate the other, to engulf or swallow the other. If the first four accounts talk of heaven, this fifth one talks of hell. But, the elements of heaven and hell are the same.

If we consider these two situations of ecstasy and horror or love and hate from the point of view we call "me," then with love and ecstasy the point of view is enhanced by the point of view. This enhancement is felt as an intensified feeling of unity.

---

16 Roberts, *The Experience of No-Self*, p. 43.

17 Happold, *Mysticism*, p. 137.

It is the feeling of joy. But it is also at the same time an expansion to embrace totality. "A single, coherent organism," "a vast expanse of photosphere." These, although contradictory, reinforce each other in a "central, immense globe of brilliancy." The dance of the center is portrayed as "a central immense globe of brilliancy." If one tastes such love but once, the rest of one's life is spent seeking yet another taste.

But, if that is heaven, then it is also hell. Seen from the point of view of me, the point of view seeks to overcome the point of view in a moment of aggressive separation. But there are not two viewpoints. There is just one torn against itself. And so there is a sinking vortex of terror as though one were slipping into a bottomless quicksand of annihilation. It is no accident the same saints who knew the glory of heaven so often succumbed to the terrors of damnation. Nor is it an accident the lover who can raise us to such heights can also dash us to such depths.

To show even more clearly the same elements are in heaven and hell let us use the me-as-center terminology: love and ecstasy, that is, heaven, is *me*-as-center/*me*-as-periphery, whereas horror, that is, hell, is me-as-*center*/me-as-*periphery*.

Mysticism—The Poetry of Ambiguity

Returning to St. John's poem, we can see he puts poetically what we have said in a stumbling way with our cumbersome and pedestrian phrases of me-as-center/me-as-periphery, awareness of, and so on.

> O living flame of love,
> How tenderly you wound
> And sear my soul's most inward center!
> No longer so elusive,
> Now, if you will, conclude
> And rend the veil from this most sweet encounter.
>
> O cautery that heals!
> O consuming wound!

O soothing hand! O touch so fine and light
That savours of eternity
And satisfies all dues!
Slaying, you have converted death to life.[18]

The "living flame of love" is that light brilliant yet not blinding; fierce yet so gentle; awe inspiring yet so full of love. "Tenderly wound"—this schism at the heart of our very being in the "most inward center"—is a tender wound, both inspired and soothed by love. It promises all because, St. John says, "Now if you will conclude and rend the veil from this most sweet encounter." To rend the veil is to take away the last separation and allow the meeting to become union. There is just one more veil. Take it away and "consummate bliss will come." But there *is* one more veil, one infinitesimal separation, and it is the wound.

In the second stanza St. John speaks of "cautery that heals." Cautery is red hot, it sears the flesh, but only to heal. In the torment of the wound is the sear of love's cautery.

"Slaying you have converted death to life"—in yielding the center, we die to the center, and therein find our life.

Full Circle

"God loves simple things because God is the simplest of all." We have now gone full circle. The human situation, a heaven that is hell, a hell that is heaven, so full of love and hatred, promise and disappointment, struggle and consummation, delight and disgust, has its origin in such simplicity.

We are separated from the ground of our being, which is awareness. Pure, simple, without blemish or stain. But, by being aware of this we fall from grace into a duality in which even the struggle, even the wish, to return is a barrier. Does it not

18   Brennar, *St. John of the Cross*, p. 163.

143

say in the Bible: "So He drove out the man; and He placed at the east of the garden of Eden the Cherubim, and the flame of the sword which turned every way, to keep the way of the tree of life."

We are whole but we seek our wholeness, and in the search we are doomed to an endless journey. Behind us is the whirling sword of ecstasy and horror. To guide us on our way is the star, which, while guiding, recedes, while promising, betrays. When we are young we taste again the glories of Eden, we are smitten by love, and some seek through love, union with the beloved or samadhi to regain the lost paradise.

Others run after the promised land, reaching out for the Holy Grail, wanting to grasp, to pin down in dogma, ritual, in the sacred word of scripture, in the fanatic pressure of the good which is certain and so dead. They see in the false idol of "being" a security that "being," in its evanescence, can never contain.

But, then there is Zen. What are the aim and practice of Zen?

Chapter 9
The Method and Aim of Zen

Strictly speaking, we cannot talk of an aim in Zen. True nature, being beyond all division and separation, is complete and lacks nothing. Anything that we do, even so much as focusing awareness, takes us away from this wholeness. The aim of Zen is to see that it has no aim. It is somewhat like the saying of Christ, "Consider the lilies of the field how they grow, they toil not neither do they spin, yet Solomon in all his glory was not arrayed like one of them."

Therefore, to see there is nothing to be done is both the method and aim of Zen. To see there is nothing to be done is not the same as doing nothing. On the contrary, to do nothing is already to do something. To verify this apparent paradox one simply has to try to do nothing for a few minutes. To see there is nothing to be done calls for long and dedicated training. A Zen story might help one to understand this.

A monk said to a brother monk, "I went to my teacher with nothing, I came away with nothing." The brother monk asked, "Then why did you go to your teacher?" The monk replied, "How else could I know that I went with nothing and came away with nothing?"

Some might feel that to say there is nothing to be done is pessimism, but that is not so. If one believes there is something

145

to be done but feels that one can never do it, that is pessimism. In a similar way, if we believe there is something to be done and feel we can do it, this is optimism. But Zen practice needs neither optimism nor pessimism.

We are addicted to doing. Goethe said, "In the beginning was the deed." To someone so addicted, to say nothing is to be done would mean that life is meaningless. But life is meaning, just as the sun is light. In the same way that we can focus the light of the sun with a magnifying glass, so we can focus life's meaning with ideas and action; ideas and action do not create meaning any more than the magnifying glass creates light. If, however, one were to say nothing can be done, this would make life meaningless. Many social revolutions happen because the tyranny of an existing regime deprives the populace of the possibility to act, and because this deprives life of any meaning, the result is an uprising against the regime. It is therefore of utmost importance that one clearly sees the distinction between the two statements: there is nothing to be done and nothing can be done. As was said, to see into the truth in there is nothing to be done requires great effort, long and dedicated training.

Spiritual Work

That great effort is necessary has been stressed by all the great religions. Christ said, "Pick up your cross and follow me." However, the effort that we make in spiritual work is different from the effort we make when working to succeed in some worldly enterprise. The latter has underlying it the struggle to reconcile conflict in some way. A common form of this struggle is trying to reconcile what could be with what is. What "could be" comes out of imagination and gives rise to plans, dreams, and hopes. "What is" arises from the way we see things. What could be arouses hope and expectation; what is has great inertia. Bringing them together is work. Many people avoid this work simply by talking about what could be; the more a person recognizes the inertia of the present, the more likely he or she is to escape in talking, reading, or dreaming about what could be.

In spiritual work such as Zen the object is not to bring about the resolution of this type of conflict but to see into the source of conflict itself. This is like swimming against the tide. As we said in an earlier chapter, much of evolution has been toward reconciling the opposites by creating or finding a center common to them both. The evolutionary thrust is to close the mind on a center, and it is this that brings about inertia. One of the ways we close the mind, for example, is to look for certainty. We seek absolute answers. Alternatively, we try to find the good or the perfect, or try to grasp or comprehend situations and our life as one unified whole. The more solid and secure whatever it is we are grasping, the better. It is no accident that the Church was built on a rock, or that a great cantata of Bach sings of the "mighty fortress" that is our God. For most, the shifting sands of anxiety, confusion, and bewilderment are unwelcome visitors. However, it is precisely by being willing to live in this condition of uncertainty and anxiety and by being willing to surrender what we feel is valuable, without then searching for something to take its place, that we gain the possibility of seeing into the source where this confusion emerges. To stay with the anxiety and the confusion, to live in the desert of the mind, or to swim upstream calls for much discipline, and that is why great effort is necessary.

To help us see this effort from another point of view, a well-known couplet in Zen says, "He enters the lake without making a ripple; goes through the forest without disturbing a blade of grass." This is saying that we should practice without disturbing anything. But can you imagine the effort that it would take to enter a lake without making a ripple, to go through a forest without disturbing a blade of grass?

Divine Discontent

I am sometimes asked, "People choose to work so hard day after day in meditation and doing long retreats. Isn't time better spent doing something else?" This question comes from a misunderstanding, from the belief that "I" decides to practice Zen, but "I" does not. The practice of Zen is the last thing "I" wants, because in a way it spells the end of me.

Zen is for the desperate. It is worth mentioning that the word desperate comes from the Latin *desperatum*, "without hope." The personality lives and feeds on hope, the hope for something that can be experienced, grasped, and known. For the desperate person hope has run out that something one can experience can give the ultimate fulfillment that one knows is possible. When hope for something runs out we are no longer afflicted by the disease of "tomorrow": tomorrow everything will be different. When we are cured of the disease of tomorrow, that which sustains all, which is beyond today, yesterday, and tomorrow, can arise. This arising first comes as a longing, but this time for something indefinable, a hope for something without boundaries or form. It is this divine discontent that drives people to meditate and to undertake the arduous journey of awakening. All the time the personality chatters, complains, protests, and resists. But more and more it succumbs to the opening power, which at first can even be seen by the personality as dreadful, threatening, and even violent. It could well be said, therefore, that people do not choose to do spiritual work; it is spiritual work that chooses them.

The Idolatry of Practice

Many people retain the hope for awakening as some type of transcendent experience, and it often drives them to sit. None of us starts with a pure mind. But, gradually, with practice, the absurdity of hoping for awakening as an experience becomes apparent. Furthermore, if it is only this hope that is the driving force, people will not stay long in the practice but will give it up, saying something is wrong with the teacher, the teaching, and so on. Even so, sometimes a person who is very ambitious will persevere. Awakening then becomes another idol, with all the problems inherent in idolatry. It is a very subtle type of idolatry because it is self-sustaining: the meditation sustains the idol and the idol sustains the meditation. One can recognize this in the same way that one recognizes any other type of idolatry. The person becomes rigid and intolerant of other ways and of other teachers. The person adopts an attitude of superiority and is compelled to preserve the minutiae of practice—the posture, the ceremonies, the forms, and so on.

Following the Breath

Zen uses the practice of following the breath. Someone may well ask, "Is not following the breath doing something?" It must therefore be stressed that the practice is to *follow* the breath, not to control it or to observe it. Instead of saying one should follow the breath one could say one should allow the breath to breathe. An illustration may clarify what is meant by the word allowing.

Suppose a neighbor were to ask you to look after her children for a couple of hours and you agreed. When the children come you could take one of three different courses of action. You could say, "Well kids, you can do as you like; just don't bother me!" You could get in there and say, "Don't do this! Stop doing that! Do this!" and so on. The first course would be to abandon responsibility. The second would be to try to control. The third would allow the children to play. This "allowing" is not active, since you do not interfere. It is not passive, since you are present with the children; present not merely in a physical way, as you would be if you had simply abandoned responsibility, but in a total way. It is like a cat sitting at a mouse hole. It appears to be asleep, but let the mouse show but a whisker and the cat will pounce. It is only by allowing that one truly understands what allowing means. In Japanese this practice is called shikantaza, or just sitting, and is recognized as being the highest form of sitting.

By allowing the mind to fluctuate, basic unity shines through. These fluctuations are fluctuations of awareness, movement of awareness of to awareness and back; or from focused to unfocused awareness. Allowing is presence or pure awareness, neither focused nor unfocused, neither contracting nor expanding. This pure awareness is, so to say, what fluctuating awareness is "made of," it is the substance of fluctuating awareness. It is lost sight of through the fluctuations from which content and experience arise. Allowing is a shift from the content away from experience to experiencing itself.

The danger of misunderstanding is great here, because it is a condition that is very similar in appearance to pure awareness but is quite different. It is the condition of awareness of awareness. Many people practice what they consider to be shikantaza, but they are really doing something quite different. Shikantaza, done properly, is to allow the mind to fluctuate. However, instead of allowing the mind to fluctuate, these people sit aware of being aware. It is a form of staring, of staring at the reflection of the mind in the mirror of the mind.

Zen masters call this sitting, because often a torpid, listless state of mind accompanies it, dead void sitting or "sitting in the cave of phantoms." The practice, awareness of awareness, can, if done intensely and with dedication, lead the mind to high states of samadhi through a marriage of the opposites, and many ascetic practices are devoted to enhancing the marriage of the opposites. However, in Zen practice, samadhi by itself is a dead end.

Buddha himself repudiated samadhi as an end in itself. At the age of twenty-nine he left his family, friends, and possessions and went into the forest as a *sanyassi*, or "homeless one." He encountered several teachers who taught him samadhi practices, and he was able to perfect himself in all of them. However, he abandoned them and continued with his search, saying these practices would not lead us out of bondage to suffering, which arises through the inevitability of sickness, old age, and death.

Many beginners find it almost impossible to accept that allowing by itself would make any difference. An analogy might make the idea more accessible. Not so long ago artists who painted in oils used paints that had turpentine as a base. When they wanted to clean their brushes, or if it was necessary to clean paint off the canvas, they used pure turpentine. An artist could, for example, leave a brush overnight after having painted and find in the morning that the brush was stiff and useless. By dipping it into turpentine, after a while it would become malleable and usable again. Just as all the colors, all the shapes, all the beauty and harmony of the paintings had turpentine as a base, so all experience, all that we know, remember, imagine, all that we see, hear, smell, taste, and feel, all our thinking, all our emotions, have awareness as a base. Consciousness, with the help of language, is hardened or crystallized awareness. By dipping consciousness in awareness, by allowing the mind to fluctuate, the mind's hard unyielding quality is dissolved and it becomes flexible again.

Being One with the Breath

To understand the practice of following the breath it is as well to understand what a Zen master said: "If you are one with a speck of dust you are one with the whole world." It is not being one with the breath that is important so much as not being identified with "I." In Zen practice the breath has no magical properties, and one should not feel that following it has any special importance. It is precisely because it has no special properties that the breath is chosen. In our everyday life we are addicted to "I." To be one with the breath is to break that addiction.

There is a difference between being one with something and identifying with something. To be identified with something, "I" must be present. When "I" is present there is a feeling of restlessness and agitation. To be one with something, we are still involved, but without the "I." There is a feeling of basic calmness and peace. Furthermore, when we are identified with a situation, we are concerned about its result; when we are one with a situation we are concerned with the process.

The more we believe that some situation or other will enable the center finally to emerge into consciousness, the more we become identified with that situation. When we feel we are finally going to grasp "it," through some love affair, some victory, some acquisition, we feel energized. But this energy comes out of an illusion, and eventually we have to pay for it in bitterness and disappointment. To be one with the situation is to have gone beyond this search for finding the center in experience.

To go beyond the search is not to abandon it. Ambition, for example, is one of the most common ways to give expression to this search. An ambitious person is one who is sure he will find "it." One might be sure that one can find "it" in wealth, position, or knowledge, but one might equally well be confident in finding "it" in some spiritual work. It is ambition nonetheless. But to retire from life, to try to avoid situations in which ambition is manifest, is not the way. Neither is the way to humble oneself constantly, to negate one's desires, hopes, and dreams. It is to see into the ultimate contradiction of seeking wholeness in experience.

The Main Obstacles to Following the Breath

In the first place, one must remember that the practice is to follow the breath. As the breath goes out, there is just an outbreath. When the breath goes in, there is just an inbreath. Some people, however, have to try to control the breath by trying to prolong it, deepen it, make it more rhythmic, have it come from hara, and so on. Others simply observe the breath. To follow the breath means neither the one nor the other. It means to be one with the breath; not, moreover, to be one with the idea of following the breath, or with the idea of the breath.

152

The idea of following the breath is to look on it as a technique, a way of accomplishing something such as pacifying the mind, coming to awakening, absorbing cosmic energy, or attaining some mystical state. People may be concerned about whether they are doing the practice right, whether they are doing it well. They ask how long they have to do it, and what is next. It could also mean they do it because someone has prescribed it as a Zen practice, or because they think it is a good idea. If they just continue to follow the breath, eventually all these thoughts will fall by the way.

To be one with the idea of the breath means to imagine the breath coming in through the nostrils, down the trachea, into the lungs, and so on. Alternatively, one imagines the numbers while counting them, or using the numbers as a mantra. This is being one with the idea of the breath. It is sterile. But these ideas, too, eventually will go, provided one is sufficiently earnest and alert.

What to Do about Thoughts

It is not thoughts that are the problem, but what underlies thoughts. Our very being is contradictory, and conflict is an essential part of our makeup. There are always two ways of seeing a situation, and these two ways are at war with each other. This may seem unbelievable, but it is so. It is like people who have multiple personalities but who are unaware of the fact. Just before the leap from one way of seeing things to the other, tension builds up because here the conflict between the two ways of seeing is at its greatest. Thinking is the way this tension is relieved. It is something like what one sees at a petroleum refinery: chimneys have flames coming out the top; these flames "flare off" the impurities. Thoughts "flare off" the tension.

Our practice is to see into this process; to see it directly, not simply to agree with some idea about it. When we do this we can stop using thought in a negative way and instead can tolerate the tension that ebbs and flows with the inner fluctuation of the mind. This fluctuation is like another, deeper breathing. One allows this breath to breathe also. Being carried away by the stream of thought is part of the allowing. One will wake up naturally in the stream carrying one off, and now it will be possible again to see the buildup of tension and to stay present again. Many people use force of one kind or another to bring the mind under control. These forceful methods depend on focusing the mind; and as we saw earlier, focusing the mind is but half of the undulation.

This answers a question that many people, particularly intellectuals, ask, "Does one have to stop thinking to practice Zen?" We do not have to stop anything. But we must be ready to allow things to give us up. A man complained to me that he drank too much and asked how he could stop. He was told that drinking is his practice. When he drinks he should do so consciously. In that way he would be ready for the time when drinking was ready to give him up. It is impossible to sin consciously.

On the question of giving up thinking, a teacher said, "Think the unthinkable!" Another way of saying this is, "arouse the mind without resting it on anything." Koan practice is a way of arousing the mind. It is a way of thinking the unthinkable. A well-known koan is the sound of one hand clapping. In full, the koan says, "You have heard the sound of two hands clapping, what is the sound of one hand clapping?" The sound of one hand is unthinkable. But nevertheless what is it?

Concentration

Concentration is an extreme form of focusing. The tension that we spoke about comes because that which is fundamentally whole and indivisible is divided against itself. All the functions of life, including consciousness, arise out of an attempt to rediscover unity. There are two ways of concentrating. The first is to try to eliminate from awareness all that is distracting, all that creates conflict. The second is to maintain a steady mind in the midst of distraction.

To concentrate calls for energy because we have to overcome the inertia of the mind. Inertia is another way of trying to rediscover unity. Repetition and habit of mind create inertia, and inertia in turn creates habit of mind. With inertia and habit, novelty, which would disturb the mind, is avoided. However, the unity of inertia is an island in the midst of a raging sea, and, moreover, it is a dead unity, although paid for at a very high price.

To rediscover original unity, which is alive, vital, and creative, this inertia has to be broken up, and to do this, habits of mind must be overcome. For many people, this calls for great concentration.

Meditation

Another equally potent way to break up the inertia of the mind is through meditation. Concentration starts, so to say, from the periphery of the mind and goes to the center; that after all is what concentration originally meant: with (*con*) center. Meditation starts at the center and goes to the periphery. When we meditate on a theme, more and more is integrated around this theme. Concentration relies on the magnetic power of the center. Most of us have read of this power in books about the martial arts, where it is called ki or chi. Meditation, on the other hand, relies on the magnetic field, so to speak, that surrounds the center. It is like the field that surrounds a magnet, which becomes apparent when iron filings are sprinkled around it. It is this field that enables the mind to establish new patterns, order, and hierarchy, and experience vital ingredients in the creative process.

The Inertia of Words

Developing power and enhancing the integrative field of the mind are only aids to break up the inertia of the mind. To understand this more clearly it is well to remember what we said about words and their being one of the main contributors to inertia of the mind. A word is absolute and, within a closed system, can be defined precisely. Moreover, words can be ordered according to an inflexible and absolute set of laws called logic, which rigorously excludes all contradiction and all uncertainty. This absolute and precise quality is like steel in reinforced concrete, and it imparts security and confidence to the person using words, giving that person the feeling of being right in what he or she says. Words dampen out the fluctuations of the mind and so give a measure of peace. They also act as a filter by which consistency and persistence are maintained. With meditation this concretelike quality is dissolved to some degree, allowing new patterns to emerge, and so it is possible for flashes of fundamental unity to shine through as original insights.

To achieve this dissolution we must be ready to let go of the demand for security, peace, and certainty. That is something many people do not understand. Zen is not a form of relaxation. Nor is it a direct road to peace. Many find that after practicing Zen for a while they begin to experience agitation, fears, and anxieties, sometimes anger and depression, that they did not have before. This happens because the inertia of the mind begins to crack. However, with the opening of the mind also comes a deep joy and a faint but real bubbling of new life. Unfortunately, because the fears and so on are on the surface and this new surge of life is in the depths, and because we are more susceptible to what is on the surface than to what is in the depths, fears have more immediacy and therefore are more obvious than joy. In turn, therefore, people may well stop practicing under the mistaken notion that they are doing something wrong, or the teaching is wrong, and so on.

Meditation might well include thought experiments or the exercises like those given earlier in the book to help you gain understanding. To do these exercises you may have found it necessary to use effort to overcome the inertia of the mind. You may have found the inertia such that you preferred to skip the exercises instead of putting out the necessary effort. However, if you do persevere, these exercises can help to some degree to break up the inertia and so help dissolve the concrete quality of the mind. However, once the exercises have made their point they should be discarded. They have no value other than as aids.

In Zen also one is often compelled to really examine closely what is being said, not in terms of what the words mean but in terms of what lies beyond the words. For example, one might ask, "What happens to us when we die?" and the answer be given, "What happens to that question when you no longer ask it?" Or, "Is there life after death?" and an answer might be, "For that for which there is a before and after there is none. For that for which there is no before and after the question is meaningless." Or, "If awakening is all that it is said to be, why does not everyone seek awakening?" "Your question is its own answer." "What does it mean to awaken; is it from a dream to some superreality?" "We awaken to the dream not from it. The dream is the dream that the dream is real. We awaken from this dream: that the dream is real." Or lastly, "What lies beyond focused and unfocused awareness?" "The power to ask that question." These are called mondo and logic, semantics, linguistics, and so on, are of no help in understanding them, yet they are not by any means nonsensical responses.

The Difference Between
Transcendental Meditation and Zen

Transcendental meditation is a way of helping establish a surrogate center using a mantra, and so, with the definition we have given, it is not meditation but concentration. For many people this can be of great, although limited, value. Using a mantra is like putting a leader in charge of an unruly group of people. Some peace and harmony are established; however, the practice is limited because it cannot give true peace, and may even become an obstruction. A leader is only effective while he or she has authority. The mantra has to retain that authority in the face of other claimants, including the legitimate one of what we have been calling wholeness.

It might be objected that other societies use the mantra as a basic religious method, and if it is good enough for them, why should it not be good enough for us? However, we must be careful what we adopt from other cultures. Consciousness is not something that is static and the same for all. Consciousness has been evolving, and in different societies it has done so in different ways. The basic structure is always the same, because the impetus to evolution is always the resolution of conflict. Even so, trying to resolve conflict by the evolution of consciousness is somewhat like trying to bang a dent out of a hubcap. For each dent you bang out you bang in two or more.

Posture

Posture is of utmost importance in the practice of Zen, although not necessarily a particular posture. For example, some teachers stress the importance of the lotus posture, forcing people to adopt it and saying it is the essence of Zen. One story tells of a young Japanese girl who came to deep awakening even though she was bedridden and quite unable to sit in a formal posture. For anyone who is crippled or otherwise unable, it is both cruel and untrue to say that the lotus posture alone is correct.

True Zen posture is concerned with the posture of the body-mind. It is to be alert to the call, an earnest attentiveness. For most people this alertness to the call is most likely to be present if they sit with a straight back and a low center of gravity. It may be in the lotus posture, it may be kneeling, or it can quite as easily be sitting in a chair. It depends on one's anatomy. If one sits with straight back and low center of gravity, eventually one will be able to sit without using any muscles to support the body. In other words, the correct posture is, so to say, the physical counterpart to "there is nothing to be done."

Awakening

Awakening is not a high level of concentration or a form of samadhi, a fusion of the two forms of awareness. Awakening is seeing into the nature of mind itself, seeing into our true nature. It is awakening to nonreflected awareness, to knowing without content.

Samadhi should not be pursued or sought after. It is acquired, and anything that is acquired can be lost. One must not allow the good to stand in the way of the best. To see into the nature of mind is to see, as Huang Po, whom we quoted at the beginning of the book, said, "There is only One Mind and not a particle of anything else on which to lay hold." Another way of saying this is that our true home is samadhi, so why strive for it? A Zen master put it this way, "To understand such a matter you have to be such a person; since you are such a person, why worry about such a matter?"

Moreover, awakening is not some supreme integration of the mind, some complete understanding. There is a widespread belief that an awakened person has access to deep and final wisdom either through an all-embracing understanding or because he or she can tap a higher stratum of consciousness. That is not so. Integration, understanding, this search for deeper wisdom is still the lust of consciousness, but freedom is to go beyond consciousness and its lusts.

Faith Is Awakening

Some people ask, "If that is so, what is the value of awakening?" Awakening has no value; it has no use. But this no-value, no-use must be meditated on. It is like faith; faith has no use. Someone said, "If faith then faith." Many who are struck by calamity complain and say, "But why should this happen to me? I have had faith in God and God has let me down." But faith is not faith in God, or Christ, or Buddha, although these may be expressions of faith. Faith in something is the drug that keeps all asleep. It

159

is like a sword kept in its scabbard. True faith is the sword held high. When one earnestly heeds the call without giving it form, this is faith and this is awakening.

As most people know, to awaken to true faith it is necessary to turn inward, but few really understand what turning inward really means. Often, when speaking about it, people point to their heads or their chests implying that inward is in the interior of the body, or head, or brain. At a more subtle level inward is into thought, or into the mind or the subjective. Outward, on the other hand, is outward to the world, to things and others, to the objective. However, the description of the human condition that we gave earlier shows there is no inner and outer. Turning inward to the subjective is to trap oneself in the subjective, which is no less deadly than to turn outward to the objective. All of our life is knowing something. What is this knowing something, that is turning inward?

To ask the question, "What is this knowing something?" one must distill knowing from all somethings. To do this one must leap the great divide, that primal separation, which all our knowledge, all our naming and logic, seek to protect us from. Many people draw back when they realize this, fearing a kind of madness. They fear that it means entering an autistic, solipsistic state; but Zen is neither autism nor solipsism. Solipsism says that the world is a product of my consciousness, but Zen says that my consciousness is also a product, and we must go beyond consciousness. Zen, furthermore, is not a form of idealism either, as this word is understood in philosophy, although some other types of Buddhism are. Idealism is dependent on the idea. Ideas arise when awareness is focused. Idea is but a viewpoint, and we must go beyond all viewpoints, even beyond the mind itself. In Zen "mind" too is empty. In one koan a monk asks the master, "My mind is still not at peace. I beg you please give it peace." The master says, "Bring me your mind here and I will give it peace." The monk replies, "I have searched for my mind and

160

cannot find it anywhere." The master says, "There, I have set it at peace."

You will recall the story of ten people who had to cross a river. It was quite a dangerous operation, and when they got to the other side, one of them suggested a count be made to ensure that no one had been lost. When one person finished counting it seemed there were only nine. Another tried, and again there were only nine. The tenth person, the one who cannot be counted, is mind.

Psychotherapy and Zen

This can give us an insight into the difference between psychotherapy and Zen, because psychotherapy is concerned with the forms of the mind, whereas Zen is concerned with the fact of the mind. Forms of the mind are ideas, memories, thoughts, emotions, and so on. By the "fact of the mind" is meant that the mind cannot be reduced to anything more basic such as brainwaves, mental energy, archetypes, libido, reflexes, and so on. Mind is mind, mind is the tenth person.

There can be no conflict between Zen and psychotherapy except when the therapist believes psychotherapy is an extension of, or a substitute for, Zen. Eric Fromm committed this error in the chapter he wrote for the book *Zen and Psychoanalysis*.[1] He said that Freudian analysis and Zen had fundamentally the same goal. A Zen teacher can make a similar error believing that Zen is a substitute for psychotherapy.

---

1   Erich Fromm, D. T. Suzuki and Rich DeMartino, *Zen and Psychoanalysis* (New York: Harper Colophon Books, 1960).

Zen and the Tradition of the Via Negativa

According to the Christian via negativa, God is beyond all attributes and therefore can be known only through negation. However, there is still the belief that God is. On the other hand, Zen goes beyond is and is not. A form of Hindu via negativa says, *Neti, neti* ("not this, not this"). One rejects every attribute until only reality remains. Zen says to go beyond that reality also. Even to talk about going beyond is misleading, because it is still talk from consciousness. Insofar as consciousness is a creation, that which creates it cannot be beyond consciousness.

A Zen story has a bearing on this. A monk asked a master, "What happens when there is nothing left?" "Throw it out," said the master. "What if you cannot throw it out?" asked the monk. "Then carry it out," said the master. Even nothing is something.

Awakening and the Brain

This naturally means that we cannot understand awakening as an activity of the brain. It has been said, for example, that awakening has something to do with the activities of the right and left lobes of the brain coming together. It might well affect the way the brain functions, but it is in no way the result of brain activity. As we have said, awakening is to go beyond the belief that I have to be something to know and to know something to be. The belief that awakening is dependent on the brain in some way comes from the belief that we have to be something to know, to be a brain, for example. Dogen, the great Soto Zen master, came to deep awakening on hearing his teacher admonish a monk, "Drop body and mind!" In other words, drop both of the above beliefs.

Fear and Loneliness

Fear of solipsism, of an enclosed autistic world, has its counterpart in loneliness, where the person is afraid of the very openness of his or her true nature. This always includes a strong element of fear of loneliness, of being alone. The word "alone" comes from two words: "all" and "one." Two well-known sayings are "fear God and dread nought," and "the fear of God is the beginning of wisdom." This fear of God is the fear of being all one. It is the gateway to freedom. Christ said, "Fear not, 'tis I." This I is not the small limited viewpoint; it is all one. Thus the fear one has when one is alone is the fear of Oneself.

Someone might object, saying, "You say we are all One, and yet you are separate from me, you do not have my thoughts, I do not have yours. How can you say we are all One?" We can use the following analogy by way of reply. Suppose there is a bell tent. Inside the tent is a light. The canvas of the tent is pierced with many holes through which the light shines. Some are big holes, some small; some face north, others face south; some are at the top of the tent, others at the bottom. Each is unique. From outside the tent there are many holes, yet inside the tent the light is one.